STILL,
I THRIVE!

STILL, I THRIVE!

24 Lessons on How to Pivot and
Evolve During an Unexpected Crisis

PK KERSEY

publish
your gift

Special discounts are available on bulk quantity purchases by book clubs, associations and special interest groups.
For details email: sales@publishyourgift.com
or call (888) 949-6228.
For information log on to www.PublishYourGift.com

This book is dedicated to all those we lost in 2020.

Table of Contents

I Can't Wait Until...

PK Kersey

How many times have people said this? How many times have you heard this? Better yet, how many times have you said this? I know I have said it quite a few times. "I can't wait until the weekend!" or "I can't wait until summertime!" and of course the all-time great, "I can't wait until my birthday!" For some reason, I consistently assumed the future offered something better than what I was presently experiencing. I was always looking to the future although I did not make any changes or adjustments so that my future would be better.

The biggest reason for my disappointments was that I worked for the government in a position for which I received no joy, excitement, or fulfillment. Yes, I was one of those individuals that hated their jobs but still arrived there every Monday at 9:00 a.m. SHARP! Well, maybe not sharp, but sometime Monday I got there.

In 2017, after 25 years of employment, I ended up leaving and starting my business, That Suits

You, a nonprofit that provides professional wear and training to deserving individuals. Anyone who has their own business knows how busy, stressful, and tiring it can be. So even though having my own is extremely rewarding, it also added a lot of pressure to my life. The process of making connections, building programs, and collecting and distributing clothing became very challenging. However, as we put in the work and as 2017 turned to 2018, we began to gain momentum and build a brand. We established solid connections with media, magazines, schools, apparel companies, etc. I would often say to myself, *I can't wait until this part of the business is over so that I can relax a little.* Or *I can't wait until I can hire more people to assist!* Toward the end of 2019, things seemed to be looking really good. Connections were solidified. Several huge contracts with New York City Department of Labor and other private job training organizations and a number of college commencement speeches were all lined up. When New Year's Eve came, I said, "I can't wait for 2020 to get here!"

Wow! Little did I know what 2020 had in store for me. I am not sure anyone knew what to expect from it. It came in like any other year, no big deal. Typical resolutions for everyone. Typical sayings, "2020, the year of plenty!" and "2020, the year of many, many, many!" You know how people do. I couldn't wait to start the sessions so I could expand my business and increase financially. Then, as fast as the year came in, the bad news started—rumors of a war and the death of NBA legend Kobe Bryant, his daughter, and others in the helicopter crash. I was like, "Wow, that is terrible and unbelievably sad." But personally, I still felt great because I had lots of business and I could not wait for the all-boy's trip to Miami that was coming up in March for the celebration of one of my best friends' fiftieth birthday.

As February came in, the US began to hear about this new virus that had started in China but was now affecting people in the United States. Having lived through AIDS, SARS, swine flu, and other viruses, I did not feel there was a threat to my life or those I knew personally. As we entered March, things became more and more severe, and more deaths started being reported. Even though all of that was happening, I still believed it would all blow over. My boys and I packed all of our things; we were excited for our long-awaited trip to Miami. We were going to have a great time, golf, take in a Miami Heat game, visit the beach, and just enjoy the fellowship. But on March 11, 2020, everything changed. When I say everything, I mean everything. The NBA canceled their season, and other sports followed. Our trip was in jeopardy because of lockdowns and we eventually had to cancel it. Schools, companies, and organizations closed down. As a result of our partners' businesses being closed, all of our contracts with them were canceled. All of my speaking engagements were postponed and every single financial contract I had for 2020 was gone. Friends that I had known for over 30 years were dying or sick. I have never seen the outlook of a year change so fast or so dramatically. In a matter of days, I went from having planned out my best year ever in business to not knowing where my next check was coming from.

Over $100K in contracts all gone. Just think about that. I often liken my personal experience of being a business owner to a lion in the wild vs. being an employee to a lion in the zoo. A lion in the zoo would get fed whether they roared or not. The lion in the jungle had to really work to eat. As an employee, I would get paid no matter how much or how little work I did. But, as a business owner, I was not going to eat without contracts or business. I began to experience some lonely, scary days because I had no income to take care of my family. Also, my 95-year-old uncle (who I have learned so much from) was hospitalized in February 2020 and being his proxy added additional responsibilities to an already stressful situation. I had to handle his daily needs (shopping, care, etc.) as well as his finances, so the walls were really closing in on me. Anyone that has the responsibility of taking care of a loved one knows the commitment, love, and focus that it takes to do it and to do it effectively. There were so many days where I felt I had nothing left in me.

As men, we are expected to have all the answers, to fix anything that is broken, to change the tire, and to open the jar of mayonnaise. All of that is great, but I think I had reached a point where I was totally empty. By nature, I am a giver. I love to help and support people, but 2020 seemed to test me like no other time. At the beginning of each month, bills were due for me and my uncle. I am a very proud man; I get that from my dad. I never like to ask anyone for anything. However, with my finances being stretched, I did not know where to turn. I had three sources of income and all three were unavailable. Trying to get through to the unemployment office in New York was almost impossible. I had no choice but to ask some of my closest friends to assist me. I felt so low doing that. It took everything in me to ask them. For two consecutive months, I borrowed over $5,000. And not only did I borrow that money from them, but I had no clear plan as to how I would pay it back! I have to say my friends came through for me. I will forever appreciate them for that. They all said that because of my character and integrity they wanted to assist me.

I appreciated their words and support, but I said to myself, *I can never get into another situation like this where I became dependent on someone else.* I made a promise during the pandemic, during that chaos, during everything that was going on, that I would make better financial decisions and better position myself to protect against similar situations. People always vow to do better when things happen or tragedy strikes, but often fail to follow through. Well, I said, "That's not going to be me!" There is something to be said about having your back up against the wall. I get a certain energy when I feel trapped or in a jam. Some of my best ideas have come to me in those situations. So, although I didn't like the position I was in, I felt a strong desire and energy to change it.

The first thing I had to do was change my thinking. Change your mind and the body will follow. Instead of always saying I can't wait for this and that, meaning that I really looked forward to those things, I started saying that I can't wait for this and that, meaning I had to do these things right now. I would not let things get in the way or stop me from making moves to secure a stronger and better financial future.

I began to do an inventory of all my current income sources. I had TSY, income from my books, and speaking engagements. I felt those were good, but I needed to add a few more. For years, I had always said I wanted to get my real estate license. I always said it but never really went after it. Well, now I said, "I can't wait for this." I immediately went to Groupon and purchased the online real estate 75-hour course. I heard my brother Jamael (who is the co-founder of TSY) talking about how he was doing pretty well trading stock options. That was something that I heard about for years, but the idea of educating myself on the language and process of successfully trading stocks seemed to be daunting. After hearing how well he was doing and being in the financial situation I was in at the time, I said, "I need to do this now! I can't wait." I began researching more about it. I watched videos and read books for weeks and finally became a trader using Robinhood and TD Ameritrade.

Around that same time, my brother (who is also a vice-president at a well-known bank in New York City) asked me, "Have you ever thought about writing a TSY children's book?" I had never really thought about it, but the idea intrigued me. In times past I might have said, "I'll think about it" but not done anything about it because every opportunity is not for you; however, when you find one that yanks your soul, go for it with all your might! So, I told him, "I can't wait to write this children's book" and we started on it immediately. The book, *That Suits You Kid*, is a story about a young boy who wins an award and gets his first suit to attend the event.

I had always wanted to start a podcast but didn't think I had the time. When the lockdown hit, I said, "This is the perfect time. I can't wait to start this. I have to do it now." I started a podcast called *Tongue Tied*. I interviewed amazing people on Instagram and allowed them to share their stories. The podcast has shifted to a monthly conversation, *Suited for Success Conversations*, in partnership with Randall Toby, a co-author of my other books and an all-around good friend.

I love to wear t-shirts and hoodies, so I thought about creating and selling branded TSY merchandise. I said, "I can't wait to do this, I have to do this now." I reached out to my other brother Sherrod who makes amazing clothing and we got started immediately. We were able to make shirts, masks, and hoodies.

All of my ventures generated income and assisted in my pivot and financial recovery. Changing my mindset from future to present elevated my life. Notwithstanding the incredible sadness we all went through with deaths and losses, 2020 turned out to have amazing experiences and fantastic lessons for me.

We have a habit of pushing things off to the future or selling ourselves short because we believe we aren't worthy or qualified. When we do, we disqualify ourselves from so many of God's blessings and favor. Many people wish they had another day to live, another opportunity to make a change. Yet because of COVID-19 and 2020, they don't have it. If we learn nothing else, let us learn that nothing is promised. We aren't owed anything. But while we are here, we owe it to ourselves and our families to live life to its fullest. That sense of urgency has propelled my life like no other time before. As a result, I highly encourage you to:

Write that book

Start that business

Marry that person

Buy that home

Do not view any question as dumb

Take that class

Follow your purpose

Stop waiting for the weekend, your birthday, or some other day. TODAY is the most important day of your life, ACT LIKE IT!

Insinuated Superpowers

Nakita Vanstory

When the people who are close to you describe you, what do they say? I've always been described as driven, highly ambitious, and a high-level achiever with a proven track record whose work exploits are juggled with raising a family, stepping up as a community leader, and much more. But being those things to the people in your life doesn't mean you don't want others to step up and take the lead sometimes. When you're everyone's rock, everyone's go-to, then who do you turn to when you're the person in need?

It is often insinuated that people who serve others so selflessly are superheroes, which is a dehumanizing remark disguised as a compliment that slightly deflects the focus away from the toll it takes to give so much of yourself to others (i.e., a super mom). I was once referred to as both an OG professional and a parent. Indeed, people intend to praise an unbridled passion for career and buoyant ability to provide and thrive as a parent, but it's dehumanizing because it implies that our accomplishments and consistency are down to superpowers instead of the actual sacrifice, hidden stress, constant worry, resourcefulness, drive, and an unfathomable work ethic that holds it all together. If others deem you "the strong one," are you allowed to be weak? Afraid? Tired? Scared? If you're superhuman, are you allowed to be vulnerable?

My name is Nakita, and I would describe myself as fun-loving, decisive, career-and family-oriented, and resilient, but never superhuman. In casual circles, I'm Nikki. I'm a deeply passionate and ambitious person who finds joy in civic engagement, mentoring, and executing anti-poverty initiatives through my personal and professional efforts. For the last 15 years, I have provided individuals throughout the borough of Queens and surrounding New York City areas with the tools and comprehensive support they need to thrive despite the opposition in their lives. To me, community is the key to personal success. Typically, I'm the one who walks with a proverbial "S" profoundly emboldened upon my chest. I am a self-proclaimed conquering lioness, a Daddy's girl, a boss, and a go-getter that is playfully bougie with a nice blend of down to earth simplicity. My optimistic mindset of growth and confidence helped me get through life… until January 14, 2020, when much of my positivity and optimism came to a screeching halt.

In 2020, I lost my 36-year-old younger brother, finally had an imperative surgical procedure that left me on unpaid medical leave for six weeks, unexpectedly lost my father, endured the historic shutdown of New York City due to COVID-19, dove into remote work and virtual programming just three days after laying my father to rest, and helped my elementary school-aged son and college-aged daughter maneuver the world of remote learning at home, all while the dramas that defined 2020 played out around me. From my diverse block in the Bedford Stuyvesant section of Brooklyn, I experienced loss after unexpected loss, culminating in the loss of my godmother—the matriarch of my extended family. The year 2020 hurt. I barely had a chance to come up for air from one ordeal before dealing with another.

This chapter goes out to the individuals who are perceived as being "strong" or having everything "figured out." It is for those who are, willingly or not, the go-to in their family for just about everything: money, advice, a helping hand, or the proverbial SOS rescuer when someone is in distress. It's for the go-getters and high achievers, the perfectionists, and busy bees—those who are an inspiration to many even when you may not feel like being so. Hopefully, this chapter will advise those silently struggling through strife, confident the role they play in others' lives can never be reciprocated. Have you ever said the words, "I need me a me?"

It all started with a normal early morning drive to work from Brooklyn to Jamaica, Queens, on Tuesday, January 14, 2020. My 36-year-old younger brother, Tony, was in the hospital in North Carolina, suffering from severe complications from his long battle with Primary Sclerosing Cholangitis (PSC). I called around 7:40 a.m. to see how everything was going and to get an update on what the doctors were doing. I briefly spoke with my father who was by his bedside, then asked him to put the phone on speaker so that I could say good morning. I was not able to hear Tony's reply, but my father told me that he acknowledged my greeting. I took a few moments to try to make him giggle, as usual, told him I loved him, then ended the call. I told my father that I would check back in with them both later in the day. Tony, who many of his peers and classmates also knew by the moniker Mecca, aka The MECCA of Rhymes, was the epitome of a hard worker and a strong-minded individual. He was very private, caring, humorous, and always willing to help someone in need. He was one to never complain, never expected anything from anyone, and feverishly pursued his goals and aspirations.

Tony was a well-respected local recording artist and concert promoter in North Carolina and had built a brand well on its way toward global recognition, having recently received over 60,000 ringtone downloads. His rise to stardom was cut short. My father called me around 8:05 a.m. and told me Tony was gone. He had passed away 25 minutes after our last telephone call. The doctors had gone into his hospital room to do more tests and probing procedures. My father told me that Tony garnered up enough strength to decisively say "No." Tony looked at my father, gave his final signature hand gesture representing his love and allegiance to the Eastside of Greensboro, closed his eyes, and transitioned. His physical fight was over.

My younger brother's passing was the most up-close and personal encounter with death I'd ever experienced. Having to handle the final arrangements, pay for the expenses, and organize the funeral was numbing. There was no insurance policy or burial funds to tap into. Writing the obituary, making critical decisions with the funeral home, creating the program, planning the service—all while grieving—is not for the faint of heart. The pain, grief, and unexpected financial expenses created a tornado of feelings unlike any I'd felt before.

I stepped up to cover all the costs, partly because he was my little brother and it had to be done, but also because I did not want my parents stressed about not having the means to cover the final expenses of sending my brother off properly. Though sick for years, it happened so fast. Perhaps as a coping mechanism, we had not planned for the inevitable. Though I was physically and mentally exhausted, overwhelmed, and disoriented, I executed the funeral planning with creativity, eagle-eyed focus, and attention to detail. With friends and family, we managed a send-off Tony would have been extremely proud of.

The shock and fright of losing my baby brother made me make my own health more of a priority and within two and a half weeks of his celebration of life, I finally decided to get an imperative surgical procedure that required unpaid medical leave for six weeks. I was not at my company long enough for full FMLA coverage, but I had procrastinated for over three years and in light of recent events, I could not hold out any longer. The doctor advised that the longer I waited, the more detrimental my condition could be to my health. It was potentially life or death. Extremely anemic, I'd started to average the need for blood transfusions every four months. For my children's sake, I couldn't continue to put myself at risk. I had to get to the root of what was keeping my blood counts gravely low. Worried about me, and wanting to be by my side, my father and mother flew to New York City from North Carolina to make sure I had all that I needed. They wanted to keep an eye on me and make sure that I was comfortable and could safely recover.

COVID-19 was quietly brewing in the US, but no alarms were sounded, nor was there much news coverage about the virus broadcasted in February. My family and I enjoyed the quality time afforded by my work respite. On February 27, my father complained of dry mouth and small lesions on his tongue, so he went for a routine hospital visit where he was treated and sent home. His vital signs were all relatively normal with a few elevated numbers (all numbers he'd seen before) that did not raise much concern. Things were back to normal, although my father and I had trouble sleeping and would talk about Tony and life deep into the night. My father was grief-stricken, and my mother shared that he sometimes cried himself to sleep or wailed in agony while sleeping.

Not long after, on March 4, my son had a drumline performance at the Barclays Center for the NBA Brooklyn Nets Halftime show: Nets vs. Grizzles. Lunch was ordered so that my parents could eat while I dropped my son off early for show prep. I planned to circle back home to pick them up for the game. The drop off and turnaround should have only taken me about 30 minutes. My father brought the ordered lunch from downstairs. He had this piercing, eyes wide open stare as I buzzed around him and out the door. He seemed slightly out of breath. My mother and others were there, so I figured he just needed to sit down and catch his breath. Nothing unusual at all. My son was excited to have his grandparents see him perform. But even though they were all dressed and ready, it was not to be. I received a text from my mother, "Get home. They are trying to resuscitate your Dad!"

When I approached my block, there were two ambulances, a fire truck, and one more emergency vehicle, if I remember correctly. I jolted up the four flights of stairs to find my apartment filled with more than half a dozen medical personnel. I stood frozen, speechless. I will always wonder if my father had heard my voice if that would have made a difference. I rode in the back of one of the ambulances with my father as they continued attempts to revive him. My mother followed in the other ambulance closely behind. En route, I messaged the other band parents to ask for help bringing my son home after the show. At 5:00 p.m., someone came in and gave my mother and me the news.

Arrangements were made to get my father back to North Carolina. I was standing at the podium at the funeral home so shortly after I had stood in that same spot eulogizing my young brother. However, this time, my father's siblings planned the memorial service and wrote the obituary. I had neither the emotional or mental capacity to do it all again, not so soon. I did, however, take care of all of the funeral expenses out of pocket once again. The only respite was that my father's brief military service qualified him for a plot in a national cemetery. That was a beautiful surprise that left me wishing I'd taken time to look more into it when he was alive. The hospital brochure was the only reason I thought to reach out to the U.S. Department of Veterans Affairs.

The year 2020 hurt me and shook my sense of self. The pain seemed unending and set me on an emotional tailspin. Out-of-pocket monetary emergencies, professional dissatisfaction, and setbacks to personal goals and aspirations all took their toll. Yet, despite those things, I found great strength I never knew I had. I reflected on my own mortality and legacy and deepened my appreciation for friends and family. I took inventory of my circle to determine their impact and purpose in my growth and roles in my long-term joy and success. I learned how to love my family more loudly than before. I acquired a heart-wrenching understanding of the importance of having tough conversations about life and death early.

When death touched my family yet again, taking a beloved matriarch and the grandmother of my daughter, I was better able to reflect on the golden wisdom, encouragement, and boundless support she'd offered me instead of ruminating on sadness and dark emotions. I thought of how a large part of who I am professionally is due to being groomed and modeled after such an exceptional woman. Her legacy inspired so much of who I am and aspire to become. If such a strong and dynamic woman saw me as her superwoman, I decided, then watch this superhero work. I, too, need moments where I can rip the burdensome "S" from my chest and fling it across the room. Who would remind me that what I am going through is normal and part of the process? I, too, need someone that will just let me gripe, vent, and share without turning the conversation to them. Initially, I felt ashamed for feeling as I did. Unempathetically, I was reminded by someone I haphazardly opened up about my losses and heartache with that it could have been worse. They told me that God gives us no more than we can bear. As accurate as this affirmation of faith is, I felt dismissed in my moment of vulnerable expression. I stopped my emotional purge in its tracks and felt slightly guilty for my grief. I was uncharacteristically in my feelings for that millisecond and trying to open up and share. I needed to be heard and seen for the person I am, not for the insinuated strength and superpowers that blind how some handle me. I needed a safe place to temporarily pull back the curtain on what it takes to be the career-oriented, dynamic mother, one-income household breadwinner, community activist, mentor, and compassionate lover of family and sincere friends. Pain can bring forth clarity. Pain and sorrow can help evaluate what you both have and are missing from life. Pain can provide a clearer picture of who you should keep close and from whom you should distance yourself.

I draw strength from family, from being a lioness protecting her pride. My life balance is drawn from my inspirations—my humble father reminding me to take it slow; my ambitious brother whose clothing line, Stay in Faith, I have trademarked and protected; my godmother who inspired my professional evolution; my hardworking daughter who graduated on the president's list in a pandemic despite similar adversity, and in whom I see my best qualities shine through. Despite the losses and heartaches of 2020, these inspirations carried me forward, and eventually I found the strength to rise—stronger and more determined than ever to sow my legacies.

So, feel how you feel. Cry and isolate. Be un-productive without guilt. Speak your pain out loud so others might help you. Remember the good times and the legacies of those you love. An ordeal is an opportunity to analyze your circumstances and revise your habits. Curate a circle of friends and family who support your goals and ambitions. Be humble and slow down. Relish the time you have with those who matter. Have gratitude. This way, you too can build a legacy worthy of a super-hero, no matter how human you are.

Divine Provision

Nicole Washington

"Beloved, I wish above all things that thou mayest prosper and be in health, even as thy soul prospereth."
—3 John 1:2 (KJV)

It was the summer of 2019. August was coming to a close. Fall would soon be upon us. That voice inside my head kept reminding me to prepare for winter... "Winter is coming." Needless to say, I was not prepared. During that time, my mentor had advised me to read Psalm 91 out loud daily for 90 days. I did so without fail. I made the decision to move out of my apartment, and I put everything I owned in storage, except what I could pack lightly into my SUV. My life was going in a different direction. Several questions ran through my mind: *Did I really want to stay in New York for winter? If not, where would I go?* Meanwhile, my best friend who was traveling in Asia at the time made arrangements for me to pick up the spare key to her apartment from the concierge desk of her building in Manhattan. My plan was to crash at her place while she traveled abroad and strategically plan my next move. All signs were pointing to go.

You see, I moved to New York fifteen years ago and in that time I bought two houses, created three different businesses, dated the wrong men, and learned a lot of valuable lessons in between. Now, here I was self-employed, single, no kids yet with nothing but air and opportunity. All I had to do was take a leap of faith. It wasn't like I hadn't done it before. However, New York was familiar to me and I thought it held the keys to everything I wanted.

As winter approached, the days became colder and less tolerable. My girlfriend would be returning from her travels soon, and I had to make a decision. The thought of spending winter in New York weighed on my conscience. I knew I wasn't going to stay. Things were different now and I needed a change of scenery. My mind settled on Florida, so I added "Move to Miami" to my to-do list. As I prepared for my leave of absence from New York, I took care of all my important business, I had my car serviced, and I switched all important mail to my P.O. Box. It was official; my move to Florida was only a few days away. I had a few more last-minute things to take care of and I was out. I picked up some items from my storage unit, gassed up my car, checked my tire pressure, and hit the highway. I drove all the way to South Florida, 20 hours straight. I just wanted to get to my destination. My drink of choice to keep me awake was the Starbucks bottled Frappuccino from the gas station. By the time I made it, I could barely keep my eyes open. I think I slept for 24 hours before I became coherent again. Miami is like a second home to me, so I had plenty of friends to visit and catch up with.

It was now January 2020 as I began to settle in. I missed New York, but in my heart, I felt I couldn't have made a better decision. The weather was amazing, and the laid-back leisure lifestyle was just what I needed. Thank God I had set my business up so that I could work from anywhere. However, I still remember having feelings of uncertainty and asking questions like: What's next? Why am I here? What is my purpose? A subtle voice replied, "Trust God." So, in my new 2020 planner, with all its blank pages, I wrote at the top of the month of January in green marker (just so I wouldn't miss it): "Trust God." And that's what I did; I put all my trust in God. One thing I knew for certain was that He had never let me down.

The Super Bowl was in Miami and the festivities were in full swing. I went to several networking events and made some new connections. I was definitely enjoying the 80-degree weather in February. I cringed thinking of the temperatures in New York at that time of year. As the Super Bowl parties and events ended and the month of February began to wrap up, there was talk of a virus that had originated in China that was wreaking havoc on New York. The headlines said that New York was a hotspot for the virus and that the city had to be put on lockdown to slow the spread. The media outlets made New York look like a complete ghost town. Everyone I talked to said that it was a very serious matter, and that people were getting sick and dying. The hospitals were overflowing, and they were running out of space to store the bodies. This thing, this virus, COVID-19 was not a joke, it was real. Watching from so far away, I couldn't help but wonder what if I would've stayed? Would I have been exposed as well?

Soon every state was on mandatory lockdown to stop the spread. The death toll was rising, and the number of infected increased day by day. Masks were now required in some places of business, and some businesses like restaurants and bars were completely closed. As the scarcity ensued, things like toilet paper, paper towels, and Clorox wipes were nowhere to be found. It was like something out of the movies. Everything, including my business and my social life, had just stopped. I was indoors for days at a time. That part, however, didn't bother me so much because I'm an introvert. It was kind of normal for me to spend time in the house like that. But three months of complete lockdown and a contagious virus was something I hadn't experienced before. Listen, I don't have to tell you about what you witnessed and experienced for yourself.

With my business slowed to a halt, I knew that I had to do something different. I had to pivot. In that moment, I began to reflect, and I realized that God's divine provision was guiding, sustaining, and protecting me. I thought back to when my mentor advised me to read Psalm 91 out loud for 90 days, to how I followed my intuition to leave New York, to my "Trust God" moment, and to even before then of course.

You see, God supernaturally protects and provides for believer's by making sure that their every need is met to enable them to fulfill His plans and purposes. God has blessed us with His Word and His Holy Spirit, two powerful and divine provisions that help us as believers to execute His plans for our lives. By faith, I trust God to do everything His Word says. "God is not a man, that he should lie" (Numbers 23:19, KJV). God's promises are real, and we can tap into them if we believe and trust in Him. Divine provision is something that you experience when you are grounded in truth. The truth is found in the Word of God. When we are grounded in the Word of God, we are able to walk in the perfect peace of God's promises. Strength and victory become ours through Jesus Christ, the Word of God. No matter what is going on in the world's system, as a believer it will not affect you.

In case you don't agree with this claim, consider the following Scripture. The Word of God says, "…Because thou hast made the LORD, which is my refuge, Even the Most High, thy habitation; There shall no evil befall thee, Neither shall any plague come nigh thy dwelling." (Psalm 91:9-10, KVJ). When we make the Lord our refuge, His Word says no plague will come near us. That also means that no famine or drought can come upon our land. We are fully protected when we trust and believe in the promises of God. Despite the craziness going on in the world, Psalm 91 confirms God's protection over our lives. I know this to be true because in 2020 things were working and coming through for me that I know were orchestrated by God's divine favor and His grace alone. As a result of God's divine provision, the year 2020 has been a blessing.

In June of 2020, I reconnected with a friend who has been a trader of the financial markets for over 30 years. He invited me to trade live with him and his online trading group three days a week. My broker accounts were already active, but I had never placed an actual trade in my account. Nevertheless, I funded my investment account and began to trade the stock market. For six months, I followed his trades and my account grew significantly. Now I'm trading on my own with a better understanding of the financial markets. Learning to trade has been life changing. I wish that I would have invested in the stock market much sooner but like the old saying goes, "Better late than never." I consider myself more of an investor than a day trader because I just don't have the patience to sit in front of a computer screen all day. For this reason, I keep the bulk of my cash in my investment account. I call it my cash flow account, this way my money is always working for me.

My newfound knowledge of the financial markets has helped me to create another income stream. Now my money works for me! There is no better feeling when it comes to making money than knowing that your money is working for you. Consequently, I have a self-managed investment portfolio. My strategy is to invest, take profits, then reinvest. When the market is down, I buy more positions, and as the market goes back up, I sell and take profits. I trade stocks, ETFs, futures, and options. I consistently monitor and update my investment portfolio. My goal is to use the stock market to create generational wealth. In order for me to stay in the market long-term, my approach is to never stop learning. I do not rush trades, and I am not greedy. I get out quickly and take my profits. Words cannot express how excited and thankful I am to be able to say that I'm a "self-directed" investor. My money works for me! Hence, I am confident that with the right investment strategy in any and all financial assets, I will become very wealthy. With that in mind, I believe that it is pertinent that we as black people get a financial education and invest our money in the financial markets. I cannot stress this enough. If you haven't already made a decision today to learn how to buy your first stock, download the Robinhood app to your phone and create an account. Open an account with TD Ameritrade and fund it. Join a trading community; get started ASAP. Trust me, you will thank me later.

Everything I learned and experienced in regard to trading and investing in 2020 was all a part of God's plan. You see, my business slowed up, but my new business of investing is thriving. God's divine provision works all the time when we cling to Him, bring our worries to Him, worship Him, and sit at His feet. This type of trust in God brings perfect peace (Isaiah 26:3). I give God all the glory and all the praise.

As you well know, 2020 was a rough year on so many different levels, beginning with the untimely death of Kobe Bryant and his daughter, COVID-19 being released on the world, mandatory lockdowns, blatant racial injustice, social unrest, loss of businesses, unemployment at an all-time high, a rushed vaccine, and a presidential election. I don't think we have ever experienced such a crazy 365 days in our nation's history. Please correct me if I'm wrong. More than anything, 2020 was a wakeup call to us all. It reminded us to put God first in all things. To be in the world, but not of the world (John 15:19). It also showed us that our health should be a major priority and a job should be considered a temporary form of income until we can create our own businesses and investments that no one can take away. It is important that we invest in ourselves to increase our individual value, starting with our communication skills, both in writing and in person. We must develop verbal confidence so that we can speak up and speak out, and get our financial houses in order so that we can be a blessing to others. God is not glorified in poverty and lack. Above all things, His wish is for us to prosper (3 John 1:2). God wants you to prosper!

We cannot erase the things that happened in 2020. What we can do is create a better 2021. Understand that knowledge is wealth and you can take it anywhere. Build meaningful relationships with like-minded people and share what you know. Sharing and exchanging valuable information with your network is the key to getting ahead in business. Learning the skill of entrepreneurship and always being professional will bring you success. Visualize what you want to happen. Your wealth is in your thinking. Get rid of negative self-talk and negative people. Position yourself to be a financial powerhouse. Love, serve, and glorify God.

Before I end this chapter, I want to say this... let's get back to "Black Excellence." I say get back because I think we lost our way, or maybe we forgot what black excellence is. If that is the case, let me explain. Black excellence is: 1) Putting God first in all that we do. 2) How we live, speak, and carry ourselves. 3) Eating healthy and staying fit. 4) Reaching back into our communities and teaching our youth what it means to be excellent. 5) *Power-Nomics* by Dr. Claude Anderson. 6) Black philanthropy. 7) Black Wall Street. 8) Each one, teach one. 9) Getting a financial education and sharing what you know with our community. 10) Us (men and women) respecting each other.

Black excellence has nothing to do with the type of car you drive, how big your house is, or how much money is in your bank account. Let's be clear. Being considered an "Elite Black" in America or the fact that you went to an Ivy League school and sent your kids to an Ivy League school does not, I repeat, does not qualify you as black excellence if you are not proactively reaching back to the youth in our communities and teaching them how to be excellent. You more than anyone has the platform to do so. Let us hold each other accountable. If you feel some type of way by me saying this, please refer to my list above and check yourself. If you would like to get involved in reaching back, I have a youth program for young women coaching them on entrepreneurship, appearance, behavior, communication, and their digital imprint. Connect with me!

With love,
Nicole

Thank You for Being a Friend

Keisha Guilford

I started 2020 out like I start every year: Thanking God for allowing me to see a new year then running down what I want my year to look like. I don't make New Year's resolutions because I never keep them. I don't start off saying, "I'm going to give up smoking for the new year." Instead I say, "At some point, I need to quit smoking." For me that's just more realistic and a more attainable goal. I refuse to start off any new year already defeated because I know I'm setting myself up for failure.

I had so many great things planned for 2020. You know what they say, "If you want to make God laugh, try and come up with your own plans." I thought, *Yes, my plans for my business are going to really pop this year. This is going to be the year that A Little Bit of Sunshine takes off.* That was me in January, but in my gut, things just felt a little off. Come February, I was super psyched. It was a leap year and I was having an event on February 29. The timing was perfect because that day just so happened to fall on a Saturday. I got a call from one of my guests who was going to be speaking that day. He told me that unfortunately he had to cancel on me because he wasn't feeling well. He went on to explain how people were acting so nervous about this Coronavirus and he didn't want people to look at him sideways if he sneezed or coughed. We laughed it off. I told him I understood and I kept it moving. You have to understand that this was before we actually knew about the devastation COVID-19 was going to bring. Neither one of us knew that after that so many people's lives, including our own, would be changed forever. None of us were prepared for what would follow in the upcoming months. How could we be? I look back on my event and think about the low turnout I got and wonder if more people were worried about it than I was.

Then came March. It was my youngest son's birthday month. We had gone to Miami the year before to celebrate his sixteenth birthday and we had a great time. I had been planning for us to take a trip to Los Angeles, but by that time things were shutting down all over the place. I was hoping and wishing and praying that things would get better sooner than later so that we could go somewhere. But we ended up doing pretty much what everyone else was doing, we celebrated from home. So many people were saddened that they couldn't celebrate certain milestones with friends and family. Funny enough, it gave me hope and a strange sense of peace to know that I wasn't in this alone. This wasn't a fight that I was fighting by myself. All over the world, there were millions of people who were fighting the exact same fight. Millions of people were feeling exactly how I was feeling probably at the exact same time.

April came and things began to start looking a little scary. There were so many people getting sick and dying. The hospitals were overcrowded. The very things that we needed to do our jobs were in short to no supply. I work with the homeless, so I too was at risk. I was worried that because of the type of work I do and the population I work with that I might contract the virus. But contracting it wasn't the issue. It was taking it home to my children or my boyfriend who is a diabetic. I was worried… and I never worry. So, I was washing and sanitizing and masking up while praying that God allowed me to continue to do my job, stay safe, and not contract anything that I could take home to my family. I wasn't worried about me; I have a great immune system. I want to say that due to working in the type of environments that I have worked in, in addition to working with the many different populations I have worked with, my immune system is always in overdrive. I made sure that I stayed six feet away from anyone, I wore my gloves as well as my mask, and I kept it moving. I saw to it that my children had the supplies they needed to stay safe but I kept my distance from them for about a month. Finally, I broke down and went to see them because I missed them so much. I told them that I love them but I didn't want them to get sick so I'd been trying to keep my distance. This is the interesting thing about genes—you pass them on to your children. They looked at me while I was going on and on about how much I loved and missed them and didn't want to make them sick and said to me, "Mom, we don't get sick. You know that." I started laughing because they really don't. Truth be told, I couldn't even remember the last time either one of my sons had gotten sick. I haven't been sick in many years. Of course, there are times when I'm not feeling well and need to take a nap or just lay down, but it has been at least twenty years since I've gotten really sick. I looked at my boys and my heart swelled with such love for them that I thought it would burst. It really is unimaginable that these two young men who sat with me on my living room couch have changed my life so much. They gave me purpose and direction when I only lived for myself. They made me a better person. They made me into the person you are reading about today.

They are my soldiers who I know would follow me into any battle and take no prisoners. Being that I am an essential worker, that visit and conversation with them gave me so much peace. Now I could go back to doing the work that I loved.

May rolled around and one of the most important holidays for a mom was coming up—Mother's Day. Of course, Mother's Day 2020 was going to be different but it was my holiday nonetheless. I looked at my boys and thought to myself, *As much as the oldest one drives me crazy, I love him with such an intensity that it can barely be put into words.* He was my only child for nine years. I didn't think that I was going to have any more children, so all of my love, time, and energy was poured into him like a fountain. He lost his father when he was fifteen years old which has left a whole in his heart. Then there is my baby, my youngest son. He brought balance to us and made everything that much better. He's a great kid. I honestly couldn't have put a baby request in and gotten a better child. I looked over at both of my smart, funny, intelligent sons and thought to myself how blessed I was to be fortunate to have not one but two amazing sons. Once again, my heart filled with joy. COVID-19 has made me really appreciate how blessed I am to be a mother. Knowing that there are so many people out there who have lost their children makes me think that no matter how much I argue with my oldest son, no matter how much he drives me crazy thinking he knows everything, there are mothers out there who wish their children were still here to drive them crazy and get on their nerves.

I thought to myself once again how blessed I was. Blessed that I have my two sons. Blessed that they are here and I can talk to them, argue, and fight with them. Blessed that I can touch, hug, and kiss them and tell them how much I love them.

My oldest son has a son, which of course is my grandson and I love his mom as if she were my daughter. My grandson, Poppas, is actually their second child. My first grandson, Aubrey, died before he was a year old due to heart complications. Even my son and his girlfriend, in their short life span, have experienced heartbreak. I looked at my grandson and thought, *I am so blessed.* They say that tough times don't last long, tough people do.

June came around and I started to do some catching up with my friends. I usually have a very busy life and sometimes you lose touch for a while. We are all busy with our families, jobs, and businesses. I have a full-time job and I run a startup business full-time. I don't even want to get into my personal life and being a full-time mom and grandma. You can't retire from that mommy job. It isn't set up that way. COVID-19 allowed me to slow down a bit. It allowed me to remember the things as well as the people in my life who are and always will be important to me. Now, I'm not saying that my friends are more amazing or more important than anyone else's, but they are mine. They are a part of my tribe. These beautiful, amazing warriors compliment me like no other. These women have been to hell and back with me. We have gone through births, deaths, marriages, and divorces. We have gone through heartbreak, headaches, problems with our children, and miscarriages. These warrior women who I have gone into many a battle with, and who I would gladly go into more battles with, are truly amazing.

Please believe me when I say that life will throw you into many wars. It will come at you guns blazing and blindside the shit out of you. Just when you think you are making some progress, life says, "I declare war." When those times come around, you are only as good as the warriors you surround yourself with. My sisters-in-arms know me better than anyone else. Hell, they probably know me better than I know myself. My queens, my Amazon warriors, know my secrets and I know there's that are never to be spoken from any of our lips. They know the worst about me but still choose to love me anyway. They know when I'm sad just from hearing my voice, and they immediately go into action to try and make me feel better.

I have spent most of my life helping people and trying to make their lives better. So, a lot of times, I put myself on the back burner. A friend of mine said to me one day, "Keisha, you take care of everybody, but who takes care of you?" As simple as that question was, it was very powerful, and it resonated in my soul. This is the cross that I have to bear. Every one of my warriors holds a very special place in my heart as well as in my life. Most of my friendships span over twenty years and have outlasted all of my relationships. These women remind me of who I am when I get so caught up in helping other people figure out who they are. When I started my business, A Little Bit of Sunshine, they made sure to ask me all the right questions. Honestly, when I started my business, I didn't have a whole lot of direction. All I knew was that I wanted to help people. I wanted to make their lives better. I wanted to bring A Little Bit of Sunshine to the lives of the people who needed it. My friends supported me even when I couldn't fully explain to them what I was doing.

July came and all you could hear was COVID-19, COVID-19, COVID-19. I was so sick of hearing about COVID-19. I had started an internet radio show in February that aired on barsandhoops.com, but due to COVID-19 they shut things down. We finally got the green light to go back into the studio and I was excited! I can't even begin to tell you how happy I was. We got an additional co-host which was awesome. My other co-host could only come in every other Monday. I said to myself, *Hey, now you're cooking with grease.* I had a fire burning so bright inside my soul you would've thought I was a shooting star. I was thinking to myself, *People need A Little Bit of Sunshine more than ever. It's officially go time!* I was finally able to get back to doing one of the things I loved to do more than anything in the world. I was going to be able to start putting smiles back onto people's faces. I believe with everything in me that if we can help someone, we should. If we can make someone's life better, do it. A lot of times, all we really need to do is offer some kind words and a listening ear. I have dedicated my life to being the one who helps others.

August came in and we were in full swing. The show was going well. I have an amazing team. My tribe was growing and I thought to myself once again, *I am blessed.* It's one thing to know your place in the world and a whole other thing to figure out what makes you tick. When you just so happen to find people who embrace what you are creating, want to be a part of what it is that you are creating, and want to take that journey with you not knowing the outcome, that is kismet. I like to say that God is a genius. He knows what you want and what you will need way before you do. You're skipping along in life, and bam, some of the things He had lined up for you that you weren't allowed to see start to fall into place. I was rocking and rolling and I was able to start booking guests to come on the show. We started to talk about regular problems that we had or were facing prior to COVID-19 and it felt good. So many of us were just trying to win the Coronavirus battle that we forgot that there were things we had been working on. Those talks, those conversations made things feel a little normal.

October rolled in and things were looking better because bad times don't last forever. I've talked about my Amazon warriors. I started thinking to myself, *I can't be the only person who has them.* I spoke to my co-hosts and they said they have warriors in their tribes as well. So, I said, "Hey, let's make October friends month!" and we were able to invite some of our warrior friends on the show and let them join us in our celebration of life. Yes, it was a celebration because there were so many people who had lost friends and family. We needed to celebrate the fact that we were still standing. We still had our warriors, and it was awesome.

Now, here comes Halloween. I normally do not celebrate Halloween because that's the way I was raised. My mom didn't allow us to celebrate it. But when she retired and I had my youngest son and my sister had my nephew, she brought them costumes and candy. I guess that's that grandma life. Once I became an adult, I had no real interest in celebrating it. But in 2020, I thought it was a good idea to throw a Halloween party for my business. I know that lots of people actually do celebrate Halloween and I do like to dress up in costumes. I had things planned out perfectly. We were going to have it in a hotel so that our guests would have the option of renting a room. I am strongly against drinking and driving, so I hoped my guests would take advantage of that option and stay safe. Halloween fell on a Saturday, but COVID-19 shut that plan down. So, I came up with a new plan. We would dress up on *A Little Bit of Sunshine* radio and it would be a blast. It was epic! I dressed up like Little Red Riding Hood from the hood with my $54.11's (also known as Reebok Classics) on, my fishnet stockings, and my big door knocker earrings. My co-hosts dressed up like Sherlock Holmes and Mr. Incredible. It was awesome! We gave out prizes for the best homemade costumes. It's an amazing feeling to connect with our viewers and listeners. I was giving back to my people. I was letting them know, "Hey, we know times are hard for a lot of people right now, but we want you to know that we are here and we care. We care that you're in the house homeschooling and you've been out of school for 20 years. We care that you're not sure if you're even going to have a job or if your marriage or relationship can survive the pressure that COVID-19 is adding to it." These are our people. These people are a part of our village; they are a part of our tribe. They are our neighbors, friends, and family. We wanted them to know and understand that they are not alone. We take care of our own.

November came and I started to get excited. November means that December is right around the corner and I have officially entered my best season. My birthday and Christmas (aka Baby Jesus Day) is in December. I was ready. I have a Thanksgiving event every year at work so that's what I was working on. The holidays are my busy season, but I love the hustle and bustle. I love my job and I take it very seriously. I love my clients and the population I work with. I go all out to make their holidays special because I love to see the smiles on their faces. I plan every menu and workshop with the thought of making their lives better. In 2020, the food wasn't the best, but my clients enjoyed their dinners and that was all that counted.

December, hey what can I say? Queens are born in December. I reached chapter 47 of my life and thought to myself, *I am blessed*. I celebrated my birthday for a week, and it was the most fun I'd had in years. I had four birthday celebrations which included two away trips. I had a birthday show and all but one of my Amazon warriors was able to attend. I made it to my forty-seventh birthday and 2020 definitely threw me some curve balls. It made me appreciate my friends, family, and just life itself. I was able to give back to people and hopefully I made dealing with the COVID-19 pandemic a little bit better. All in all, no man is an island, and I am no exception to that rule.

To everyone who is walking this road with me. To everyone who loves and supports me. To my family and friends who love me unconditionally. Thank you for being a blessing in my life and for reminding me how truly blessed I am.

The Evolution of the Busy Bee

Tamykah Anthony

The most pressure I have ever felt as a Black female scientist came when the coronavirus pandemic of 2020 unfolded. I had always been "the trusted friendly neighborhood scientist" to friends, family, and the community as a whole, so naturally when a health crisis hit, my phone and social media inboxes were flooded with questions and concerns from people looking for reliable sources of information. Unfortunately, I did not have many answers. Even though I was a toxicologist, I was in some ways just as lost as everyone else. Being a mother of three, I had the same fears as other parents worrying about how to keep their children safe. In addition, since I had been a homeschooling mom for eight years, there were also parents reaching out for advice and guidance about homeschooling as a safer option during the pandemic. And if that wasn't overwhelming enough, I was also going through a tumultuous divorce AND in the middle of a not so pretty healing process while writing my second book, an autobiographical poetic memoir called *Diary of a MisEducated Baby Mama: The After Birth*. The events of 2020 had a profound impact on my writing.

Compounded with the uncertainty the pandemic brought was the intense emotional and mental unrest resulting from the senseless murders of innocent Black people like Breonna Taylor and George Floyd. It felt like we were all experiencing "when it rains, it pours" moments back-to-back. Everyone seemed to be searching for an outlet or a voice at a time when masks, social distancing, and quarantining prevented regular human interaction and healing conversations with friends and family. I had an amazing experience writing my book because it gave me an outlet to not only facilitate the much-needed release of childhood trauma and triggers, but to also process the current events. I had decided after self-publishing my first book that I wanted to start my own publishing company, but I wasn't really sure what the mission would be besides publishing my own books.

A few years ago, I was filling out a questionnaire for an event I had been asked to speak at and had trouble with the question: "Who are you and what do you do?" I was trained as a forensic scientist, but it just did not feel like a good summation of who I was, so I analyzed myself scientifically and wrote down everything that I did at that time. Included in the list were educator (I've taught all grades in traditional school settings and non-traditional settings), forensic toxicologist, author (at that point, I had written and published one book and had co-authored three scientific journal publications), entrepreneur and business owner (I had used my expertise as a toxicologist to create a non-toxic natural product line that families could trust called Xanthines All Natural Products and had started a camp called Camp Wakanda to teach melanated children about their innate superpowers), homeschooling mom, and a women's health educator (I had created an event called the Vagina Dialogues that was geared toward teaching women about their bodies to help them achieve optimal sexual and reproductive health and overall womb wellness). There were more bullet points on the list, but as I began to just write freely, I noticed there was something that linked all the things that I do. I was using my love and knowledge of science and community to create businesses and platforms that inspire and promote healing and wellness. So, I came up with the term scientistpreneur. Since then, that has been the most succinct way to describe myself.

As I was completing my second book and needing some formatting help, a good friend recommended J. Cerrone Smith, fellow author and CEO of Paper-Chase Publications. Not only did he help me format my book, but he also helped me brainstorm names for my publishing company and he was instrumental in the logo I designed for my company, Busy Bee Publications. Falling in love with him was easy after that, but that's a story for another time. So, why bees? For as long as I can remember, I have been obsessed with bees and their way of life. While getting my degree in forensic science, I had to take two semesters of a class called organic chemistry. Most of my classmates hated it, but I absolutely loved it and loved learning about the molecules and chemical formulas, and the lab sessions were also very interesting. In one of our labs, we learned that the ingredient used to give something a banana flavor was actually a compound called isopentyl acetate; coincidentally, this is the same compound that bees use for their alarm pheromone. When a bee is disturbed, it releases this pheromone to alert other bees of danger. I was so fascinated by this that the isopentyl acetate molecular symbol and bees became one of my tattoos.

In 2015, a few years after I got the bee tattoo, I was working at Columbia University when I developed an eye condition called polypoidal choroidal vasculopathy, an extremely rare form of macular degeneration that usually only develops in older people of Asian descent. Needless to say, the doctors were baffled since I was clearly not Asian and had just celebrated my thirtieth birthday. The eye condition caused abnormal blood vessels to sprout in both of my eyes and burst, resulting in hemorrhaging and increased pressure in my eyes. The doctors also told me that my condition was one of the most aggressive they had seen, so I started losing my vision fairly quickly. In a matter of weeks, I could no longer work so I had to leave my job, a job that marked just the beginning of the career I had been building since getting my degree. I was devastated and feeling hopeless. Not only did I lose my job, but I also lost the salary that came with it. In some ways, my sanity dwindled as well.

Sight gone. Salary gone. Sanity, questionable. For the next eight months, I endured painful eye injections in both eyes and struggled with losing my sight and not being able to perform daily functions because of limited vision. But more than anything, my spirit was in struggle mode. After all those months of eye injections, I had eye surgery to remove some of the blood in my eyes in hopes that it would help my vision. It was not as successful as planned, and my eyes continued to fill with blood, leading to random brain bleeds and a slew of other related issues.

I had heard about Dr. Sebi and his healing village in Honduras, but, at the time, I didn't have the money to pay for the flight or the cost of staying in the village for weeks to be treated. Although we are now divorced, I am grateful that my husband at the time took initiative and created a GoFundMe page in order to raise the funds. Through those donations, I was able to travel to Dr. Sebi's Usha Village in Honduras, where I was healed, and my vision returned within less than a week of me being there. For those reading this who want to learn more about my healing journey with Dr. Sebi, you will have to wait for the book release. Back to the bees!

Part of my healing regimen involved putting honey into my eyes and I truly believe that in addition to the alkaline diet, that was essential for my healing. So, the bees pretty much saved my life and that of my unborn daughter who I was seven weeks pregnant with when I went to Usha Village. I named her Usha.

The empowerment of women, specifically women of color (including myself), has been a deep passion of mine for several years. Too many times throughout my life, from childhood into adulthood, I have felt silenced or felt like my voice was taken away. One of the reasons I decided to write my two books was to ensure that I could "speak" without anyone talking over me or trying to shut me up. The more I spoke to women of color, the more I realized that they too had stories to tell and truths to speak, but there were barriers that prevented them from doing so. I wanted to remove those barriers and provide a platform for them as I had provided for myself. I wore several hats, as mentioned before, and I knew that was not unique to me. Being a mother, running a business, going to work, being a partner, taking care of self, and just navigating the patriarchal tendencies of society were all barriers. In essence, most women I knew, including myself, were "busy bees," working hard without having enough time to "smell the flowers" much less write a book, but their voices needed to be heard. One of my favorite quotes from Ntozake Shange is, "I write for young girls of color, for girls who don't even exist yet, so that there is something there for them when they arrive."

Busy Bee Publications was birthed during the COVID-19 pandemic with a very woman-centered purpose—to function as a full-service publishing salon where we understand firsthand how women often have to juggle the demands of being a "busy bee." From writing and editing to publishing and marketing, Busy Bee Publications is a one-stop shop for those looking to become published authors.

I combined my love for bees and my drive to see women win at a time when I felt like it was most needed, and the response has been overwhelmingly positive.

Coming Out Better Than I Went In

Nathan Johnson

Life has a way of disrupting our regularly scheduled programs. In March 2020, just as COVID-19
was starting to pick up steam in the media, my lady
and I went to Miami to celebrate her birthday. At
that time, I thought it was an overseas disease, only
affecting those who had traveled to the infected areas. I knew things were getting more serious when
the two-day concert I had bought tickets for was
canceled. But even with that, I was still on task
with the mission: have fun in Miami. So that is
what we proceeded to do. The weird thing is, I am
usually pessimistic, but my desire to go on that trip
had me in an optimistic frame of mind.

I really enjoy planning for trips by researching places to eat, local activities, and events. I had
scoped out a nice Greek restaurant in South Beach
and was in great anticipation of treating my palate.
The food was fantastic. We ate, shared cocktails,
laughed, and had a blast. Even with the fun times,
I had an awareness of what was going on in the

world because every now and again, I would check my social media. I saw that things up north where I am from were not the same as in Florida. Up north, they were talking about freezer trucks being present outside of hospitals to place dead bodies inside. The hospitals and the funeral homes were overcrowded. Things were sounding really spooky. I would tell my lady during the trip, "Hey, we better enjoy ourselves because when we get back, things will be different."

With the death toll rising and the many shutdowns across the world, we wondered on the flight back to Jersey whether our jobs would also be shutdown. We discussed that if things were shutting down at my job due to COVID-19, I would just go down to Maryland with her. The logic behind that was that it is less populated in Maryland where she lives, so there was less of a chance of being in contact with folks. I also did not want her to be alone during this now worldwide pandemic. That gut feeling I had was correct. My job said I was furloughed due to the global pandemic and it was off to Maryland we went. We caught the train while very paranoid about touching anything. At the time, masks were not mandatory, so we made sure to limit our contact with people. When we arrived in Maryland, we knew it was time to hunker down and really try to figure out what was going on with COVID-19. Watching the local news was starting to really amp up my paranoia. I told my lady, "This is seeming like something biblical." It had a real Armageddon feel to it, especially the term global pandemic.

I started to focus on being as on point as I could possibly be, so we decided that we were not going outside unless it was absolutely necessary. All types of information and remedies were being posted on social media. There was one recommendation to boil orange peels and spices and inhale the steam to kill the virus in your nasal passage. You guessed it. Me and my lady both almost scalded ourselves trying it out. It's funny looking back at it now, but back then I had a "whatever it takes to stay safe" mentality.

The magnitude of the situation was bringing us closer together, although we had a few challenges adjusting. We had a long-distance relationship, so we got together often; however, we had never spent more than three weeks together at one time. I knew this was going to be longer than a three week stay. So, we spent a lot of our time having deep conversations about how we needed to be on the same page as it related to our safety. It felt good to see she was in tune and took things just as seriously as I did. During one of our conversations, I remember saying, "We can't go through this and come out the same way we went in." I wasn't all the way clear on how or what was going to be different, but I knew I needed to do the time and not let the time do me.

My first step was working on maximizing my physicality. I wanted to have my body in peak condition to potentially ward off anything, especially COVID-19. I started my morning routine workouts of fifty pushups and fifty crunches, along with riding my lady's exercise bike to compensate for the lack of walking. Thankfully, Amazon was still up and running. I made sure to stock up on my supplements of black seed oil, sea moss, bladderwrack, vitamin D, elderberry and echinacea, along with my daily smoothies consisting of kale, spinach, almond milk, and mixed frozen fruit. Now that I had a lot of time on my hands, I decided to exercise my mental by learning a second language. I was told about a phone app to learn a second language, so I downloaded it and began to learn Swahili. "Habari za asubuhi" means good morning. Okay, I'm not ready to have a two-hour conversation with a member of the Dinka tribe, but it has been a fun and challenging journey so far.

Things were moving along well. Ladybug and I would only go out to do grocery shopping and laundry. I was working out regularly and practicing my Swahili. I also decided to maintain consistent contact with family and friends, especially my mom who lives alone in Brooklyn, New York. New York being such an epicenter of the pandemic put me in a real state of concern for my mom. I struggled with a feeling of guilt that I was with someone and she was in the belly of the beast fending for herself. The only thing I could do to ease the feelings of apprehension and guilt was to ramp up the amount of times we talked on the phone. I knew the fact that she couldn't go to fellowship at church was a big blow for her, so I wanted to do my best to fill that void if possible.

As the horror stories continued and loved ones were being taken away, I decided to reach out to my cousins, and we started a weekly video chat called Quarantined Cousins. We would talk about everything under the sun and decided to spice things up by playing a bootleg version of *Name That Tune*. I took things further and created my own version of *Ghetto Jeopardy*. I set the bar high but was pleasantly surprised how everyone stepped up their creativity in providing the entertainment for the Quarantined Cousins. It was rolling along and gave me a needed escape from the gloom and doom of the media and the nonsense coming out of the White House. Through staying in contact with family and friends, I received a phone call from two of my old high school homies from my old

Brooklyn neighborhood. As we were catching up and inquiring about each other's safety, the conversation took a turn into current events and the topic of police brutality toward people of color. This was sparked by the only news story that was able to shift the media coverage away from the Coronavirus—the videotaped killing of an unarmed black man in Minneapolis, Minnesota, at the hands of police. All three of us were extremely frustrated and inspired to be a part of the solution rather than just turning a blind eye.

A global movement toward police reform and accountability was in full effect and it was just as strong as the global pandemic. As we continued to reminisce, we talked about our yellow school bus rides from Brooklyn to Jamaica, Queens. We would have the whole bus captivated with our banter. Most of the time it was sports-related, but the topics ranged from girls, to fashion, to good ole yo mama jokes. One of my friends suggested that we create a format to speak up and out against the injustices we see in our community and talk about black empowerment. I suggested we set it up like the video meetings I do with my cousins. We wasted no time and agreed on having a video meeting that next Wednesday.

We invited our friends and family to join and be a part of our cyber audience. We needed a name for our new video podcast. Since it was derived partially from our old bus rides to high school, I thought that a good name would be *The Cheese-BusChat*. We decided that I would do the majority of the talking and although my mouth can go, when showtime came for the first *CheeseBusChat* I was a ball of nerves. My nervousness was soon put to rest when I noticed that most of the fifteen or so people I had contacted to be a part of our cyber audience had given me the gas face aka they were a no show. In fact, only one person tuned in for that first podcast. Instead of being discouraged by the lack of an audience, we chopped it up with our one participant. We had a productive build and got even more determined to get the word out and persuade folks to tap in with us. As the podcast began to grow, I decided to bring another friend on board. He's been my right-hand man since my early twenties. Throughout our interactions, we were constantly building on various topics and he always had a way with words, so I knew he would be a good addition and together we could keep an audience's attention.

I am pleased to say that as I began to grow beyond my introverted apprehensions and hidden shyness so did *The CheeseBusChat*. We had a growing, actively participating audience tuned in for a melanated cyber experience. Due to the climate of racial tension, we began promoting more black-owned businesses, black literature, black history, and black unity. Some in our cyber audience inquired as to why we were not trying to put our video chat on a bigger platform such as social media. I have learned that in life you must be wise and do things at the right time, and having a handle on the energy that would be present during our sharing of information and ideas was important. The truth is not everything is for everybody. You must not only guard your heart and mind but your assignments. It has been nine months since the inception of *The CheeseBusChat* and we are still rolling strong with topics ranging from child support to pyramid schemes. We continued to try to elevate and bring positive vibes to our cyber audience in hopes that they stay encouraged and determined to keep pushing during that time of Coronavirus lockdowns, masks, social distancing, and unfortunately death.

During that time of unpredictability, it was paramount that I stayed focused. I made a conscious decision to stay clear of anything that could alter my train of thought during quarantine. Even with my different outlets, there were moments when my paranoia would still get the best of me. At one point, I was fearful of taking out the garbage and checking the mail. Yes, I faced emotional and mental challenges, but I fought through each one. I was determined not to be defeated by my own thoughts and inner fears. I knew I had to shake all fear and put my trust and faith in a higher power. Sometimes we think we have to do big things to make changes; however, doing just a little bit every day and being consistent was a key factor in me being able to move forward and maintain a positive outlook in the midst of negativity.

I know that 2020 was a rough year for many. I decided to change my trajectory and focus on all the things that did go right. I could spend eternity focusing on all the wrong things in life but grasping the lessons is wealth. Learning, growing, and evolving into the best you by putting in the work will outlast any trial and tribulation. I am grateful that despite the world's temperature, I was able to celebrate my fiftieth birthday. My plan was to spend it in Africa but due to the pandemic it was postponed. I, however, was able to still celebrate. The love for my family and commemorating my fiftieth birthday with them was greater than the fear.

The pandemic death rates started to decrease but my learning and growth continued to increase. I celebrated my pre-fiftieth in ATL where I was able to see life through a different lens. Life can be progressive if you put in the work. I also got a chance to visit the place where one of the major topics that gave birth to *The CheeseBusChat* took place—Minneapolis, Minnesota. It was surreal, humbling, and emotional to stand in the same place where such a tragedy took place. The need to pay homage and respect to George Floyd outweighed my paranoia of COVID. It was a reminder that the fight for justice is not over. Although we are still in the pandemic, we are also still weathering the storm of police brutality as a people.

Though the COVID-19 pandemic is far from over, I can already say that if God allows and I am on the wake up list when this is officially over, I will indeed have come out a better, more humbled and grateful version of myself.

Lessons from a Stylist: Grace for Grief During a Pandemic

Laura "LB" Butler

The year 2020 was full of devastating heartbreak and incredible moments that I will treasure forever. In January 2020, I felt God impress the word overcome upon my heart. It came to me as I battled a chronic illness and heartbreak that left me struggling to get out of bed and function each day. I believed the word overcome meant seeking support to relieve my pain, taking steps to manage my condition, practicing self-care, navigating emotional turmoil, and finding peace in Jesus. God also reminded me that I've long been an overcomer. I turned 44 in 2020 and never imagined being "sat down," as my southern family says, because of a pandemic. While placed in a cultural, global, and social time out, we all had no other choice but to sit and face what we'd likely spent months, years, or a lifetime trying to avoid. It seemed we now had nothing but time to face unhealed wounds, pesky habits, and toxic relationships that did not serve us. I have been through a lot in my life, but the pandemic was something else.

I reside in Park Slope in Brooklyn, New York. I'm a principal clinical research associate for clinical trials that are now booming due to the COVID-19 pandemic. Besides being a professional researcher, I've had a lifelong passion for fashion, beauty, and healthy living. My signature look is rocking my goals, aspirations, and confidence! I'm the CEO and founder of In2itive Couture by LB Designs, your premier destination for style, travel, health and wellness, and biblical principles. I'm a go-getter with a passion for injecting creativity into everything I do. My skills go beyond spearheading research in labs and medical offices. I "research" styles! I love experimenting with fun new styles and trends, but I rely on classic pieces which ensure I'm ready (sassy and bossy) in minutes at the end of the day. I share my style secrets to help make others feel and look their best. My passion for helping others, combined with my love of style and self-care, encouraged me to write this chapter.

Let me reflect for a moment. I lost both of my parents in my teenage years. I have been married twice and miscarried twins in 2007. I then dealt with the utter heartbreak of losing my best friend, Wali, in 2018. I've lost many family members and friends throughout the years, which as we know is a part of life. I'm fortunate to have three brothers; my sister, Cheryl; another sister-turned-mother figure I call Momma Callie; a brother-in-law, Abdul, who I call Baba; one stepbrother, Luck; one bonus sister, Tifah; and several besties: Tenikka, Dana, Kim, G, Ephy; and a mighty prayer warrior best friend, Maurissa. My inner circle is small but mighty. They've seen me through fearless adventures, encouraging victories, and some heartbreaking moments too. Their love and support has been critical as we are all facing the uncertainty and chaos wrought by the pandemic.

I have been in lockdown in my railroad apartment since March 2020, and even though it has been a tough time, I have made it through. I've found solace in my mornings and afternoons with Earl Grey tea with a splash of lavender or vanilla. I'm on prayer calls saying prayers and reading my daily devotionals and the Bible. I'm cooking, laughing, and making phone calls. I video call lots of my family and friends and I'm even making new friends via social media. Virtual connection has become a crucial part of daily life. I love using WhatsApp, FaceTime, or making Zoom calls. And of course I'm popping on the screen with bold or iridescent colors and statement earrings! Connecting allows me to gain strength, provide my friends and loved ones with hope, and encourage them to keep the faith and believe that everything will be okay in the end, even if things are not as we'd envisioned. The pandemic created uncertainty and disruption, but it can lead us down a new path. It can encourage us to reevaluate our lives and the energy we give to the people in it. It can help us forge a different path or generate new opportunities. We will get through this. We are TOUGH. I remind myself that no matter how difficult life is, I'm resilient and I have faith in GOD. I know WE can endure. In ages to come, the COVID-19 pandemic will be a distant memory.

Writing this chapter allows me to send you my love, encouragement, and prayers. "What doesn't kill you makes you stronger," so the saying goes. And that is more times than not, unfortunately, right to a fault. The load we carry, be it an illness, feelings of abandonment or neglect, our insecurities, our heartbreaks, a divorce, abuse, death of loved ones taken too soon, childhood trauma... and now navigating a pandemic... it's enough to bring you to your knees. It can all create a stress that sits deep inside of us. I've carried the pain of others as well. I'm empathetic with a compassionate heart. While I'm pulled together on the outside, internally I have to manage the balancing act of finding: the power to keep myself going, the strength to help others, and the ability to adapt to life's changes.

The 2020 holiday season stormed in carrying with it loads of emotions. It was the first holiday in a different emotional space. It was the first during a global pandemic. None of those were firsts that I wanted to experience ever, much less simultaneously. So, I conserved the little energy I had to make my holidays unforgettable because after all I'd endured in the first nine months of 2020, I certainly deserved it. But let me tell you, unpacking my emotional baggage has been a heart-wrenching challenge that I didn't see coming. And THAT will stop your heart. The saying, "It is what it is," holds true in this challenging season. But it's one foot in front of the other, and I've never been so aware of the blessings that I do have. I'm reminded of God's strength within me.

The beginning of 2020 was seemingly uphill. I was enjoying my quiet time each day, working my way through reading the Bible from start to finish, prioritizing my health and nutrition to become the best version of myself, and putting effort into doing things to help me feel more like myself. I felt as though I was starting the year strong, sure that I would reach my goals. Then March came and on top of the pandemic, I dealt with one of the most painful experiences that left me broken to my core—heartbreak and betrayal. Heartbreak is more than just an emotional defeat. Many different circumstances can cause it, and that's what makes it a universal pain that anyone can understand. Sometimes the people we trust the most can end up being our worst enemies because we often trust them with the most sacred parts of ourselves.

I remember feeling uneasy and suspicious for quite some time about a guy I was dating, and while doing a little bit of digging, my concerns were justified. I saw pictures on Instagram of him hugged up mid-kiss with a girl. It was the last thing my mind or body needed, especially while battling a new diagnosis of chronic pain. I called the gentlemen out on the BULL once I discovered the truth behind my growing doubts. The funny thing is, I initially thought I was unhappy with my career or something. When I look back and am honest with myself, I knew from the moment I reunited with him in early 2020 that despite a few happy months of enjoying companionship, working to give love with vulnerability, and building new memories something was wrong. The confirmation of the betrayal came just as COVID-19 was bringing our world to a halt, which left me unable to freely find refuge in the people and activities that could bring me some release. I felt stifled. My anguish was amplified. I felt emotional and physical pain seeping from every pore of my body.

The pain was familiar to me. Twenty years ago, I experienced the agony of infidelity. In that case, however, it wasn't exposed on social media because those platforms didn't exist. Now, friendships and relationships are easily formed and progress behind a screen. Men and women are more friendly, making it easier to overlook or turn a blind eye and ear to signs of infidelity. Additionally, the individual who has been unfaithful vows to do "anything" to make it better, but the next day continues to indulge with the pattern of infidelity. At that point, the relationship or marriage is sabotaged. The person experiencing the agony of the deceit is pushed deeper into turmoil. Discovery of the infidelity is besieged by horrible images online and it can leave you overwhelmed with anxiety. So, this time around I found myself questioning God and wondering how I would overcome this. How would I survive dealing with my diagnosis and the pain of betrayal and hurt behind the scenes? Presents don't band-aid scars and the love isn't real when the intimacy is given to other women. Would I be able to pull myself together to take care of myself? Dealing with a broken heart and deception causes a deep pain and mental weight that I know has taken many to the grave. So, I'm being transparent about my journey to try to save a life today.

The reality is that both the betrayed and the betrayer should move forward. But sometimes the betrayal has been so great—multiple affairs or cheating with a friend—that recovery is much more challenging. If you can't get over the experience, you may think the pain is too great and you need to split up. Some think it's harmless or acceptable to continue relations with a lover at the end of a fling. Unhealthy repeated behavior, in my experience, leads to more heartbreak, as the affair often lingers on, threatening your well-being and causing a great deal of unnecessary anguish.

Being betrayed is terrible enough, but being betrayed twice in the same way with the same person is twisting the knife. However, there is a message of hope. Even out of extreme hurt, you can find help and learn different skills for processing the pain and beginning the healing journey to wholeness. God gave me the will to overcome and I knew that eventually I would. I started by focusing on my health. I decided to receive treatment from my pain management specialist, Dr. J. I found solace in the Word of God. I leaned on trusted friends and family. I took it one day at a time. Healing physically and mentally is not always straightforward. It has taken far longer than I would have imagined and has been in tandem with addressing my chronic pain.

The world is full of people dealing with physical pain, mental or emotional challenges, or broken hearts. Those types of personal obstacles can disrupt everything and, in some cases, prevent you from functioning and strip you of any sense of normalcy.

The most common "cure" is time and finding a treatment plan, if necessary, to address your overall well-being. A critical part of my self-care is praying for guidance, reading, and meditating on God's Word. Psalm 147:3 teaches us that only a child of God can encounter recovery since only the Christian has the right access to the Holy Spirit of God, the one who heals the brokenhearted and binds up their wounds. Healing can never come from our efforts or attempts; it comes from God. He can make us complete. He can take our emptiness or brokenness and make us into what He wants us to be. While we experience trials, the Lord is gracious. He can give our lives joy, meaning, and purpose. John 6:37 affirms that "All that the Father gives me shall come to me, and him that comes to me, I will in no wise cast out." I also find comfort in Luke 12:6-7 because those who know, love, and trust Him never need to worry that He is unaware of their suffering or that their requests for relief are being ignored. His relationship with His children is one that will never be shattered. "Draw near to God, and He will draw near to you. Cleanse your hands, you sinners; and purify your hearts, you double-minded," is a powerful reminder from James 4:8.

Whether we are healing from a heartbreak or life trauma, the process of healing, specifically getting through the pain cycle, can be one of our most outstanding teachers. In my experience, when the trauma first happens it is very jarring, like someone slapped you in the face. It's acute like death. Abrupt. Then, there is a little or a lot of anxiety around it! There's also a feeling of betrayal, and just so many feelings swirling around about how others notice our differences and what they think of us. This self-consciousness interferes with existing, monopolizing our energy that could better be used for growth. Subsequently, there's a choice: look at the pain and learn from it or avoid it—deny it or drown it in your choice of pain reliever. If you choose to go into it, you may come to realize that the pain, although uncomfortable at first, presents an opportunity. In time, it can become one of your greatest life lessons! Healing takes courage, not the kind that closes off and toughens up or becomes bitter and unforgiving or unloving... but the kind that strengthens and breathes, forgives, and heals.

Healing requires softening flexibility. It takes an understanding of the distinction between the passion that comes from within us and the pressure from outside influences. It takes a willingness to learn and grow and move forward! Thank you, my sweet loved ones whose years belie your wisdom and heart, for helping me heal at times when life's challenges have affected my mind, body, and soul. I will continue to heal and grow. I am a work in progress! I am getting there!

I overcame all that 2020 brought my way; but truthfully, I have to work each day to let go of the things that happened in the past to move forward and focus on the here and now. On the days when my anxiety is at an all-time high, on the days when I have to will myself to function through the physical pain in my body, on the days when I wonder when we will be on the other said of the COVID-19 pandemic, on the days when I feel numb and want to crawl into the bed—but God. One thing 2020 taught me was that God is present in the good times and the earth-shattering times. While I may struggle, I will always show up and take care of my responsibilities and then some. I have grown in self-awareness and have a new love for myself. I've realized that I am much stronger than I think, capable of doing things I couldn't have imagined, and able to pull myself through and overcome any obstacle with God's strength.

My word for 2021 is restoration. I'm hopeful about strengthening my relationship with Jesus, praying for good, and committing to quality time with Him each day. I strive to continually better myself as a Proverbs wife, daughter, sister, auntie, and friend. I pray for restoration with my family and friends, more love, grace, and forgiveness, fewer fights, and less bitterness and resentment. I believe in restoration with my clients. I will try my best to advocate for them, learning all I can to help them grow into the best versions of themselves from faith and fulfilment to fashion and everything in between. I'm praying for restoration in friendships. The year 2020 left me grieving the loss of companions and hopeful in the new friendships I've made. Now, it's a new year and a fresh start. Restoration is coming my way. I'm claiming it. Things might not go as I expected. "The Year of Overcoming," 2020, certainly did not. But I know that by keeping my eyes on Jesus, HIS restoration will come.

My journey toward sharpening myself in God's grace has been truly unbelievable. It has encouraged and humbled me, given me reasons to sing when I'm tempted to despair, and it has been the most helpful practice in healing. God's grace is there for me and it's available to you too. I leave you with 2 Corinthians 12:9, "And he said unto me, 'my grace is sufficient for thee: for my strength is made perfect in weakness.' Most gladly therefore will I rather glory in my infirmities, that the power of Christ may rest upon me."

Fearlessly Leading in a Fearful Time

Dakota Keyes

*"God has not given us a spirit of fear, but of power,
and love, and a sound mind."*
—2 Timothy 1:7

I held my phone in my hand in total disbelief as I read the incoming messages from my colleagues alerting me that Mayor de Blasio of New York City was about to announce a system-wide closure of all public schools. As I waited with bated breath for the forthcoming announcement which was being aired on all of the major networks in New York City and beyond, my thoughts wandered to instances in the past when mountains of snow fell upon the city that never sleeps. My fourteen years of experience as a principal of a New York City elementary school provided me with some insight into how the press conference most likely would unfold as it related to school closures. On numerous occasions, I awoke after falling asleep as mountains of snow descended upon the city, anticipating with a great degree of confidence that school would not be in session for students or teachers on the following day, only to be stunned by the decision to keep all 1,800 New York City public schools open in spite of the challenges associated with a heavy snowfall and the necessary subsequent clean up. During the past 26 years of working within the New York City Department of Education, I could probably count on one hand the number of occurrences that forced the closure of public schools throughout New York City. The 9/11 terror attacks are inclusive on this list of events that caused the largest school system in the United States to shut down. However, the deep degree of grief and sorrow engendered by that horrific event, the incomprehensible aftermath of that national tragedy, the insurmountable number of lives lost, and the complete collapse and destruction of the iconic World Trade Center merely resulted in the closure of New York City public schools for approximately 48 hours. By the Tuesday following the 9/11 attacks, all New York City public schools were open with the exception of those schools directly impacted within the Ground Zero area of lower Manhattan.

So, I didn't anticipate that this news conference would be any different. Nonetheless, I still waited with cynical anticipation as to what the script would be. Appearing visibly distraught, the mayor of New York City began to speak on Sunday, March 15, 2020, and his words jolted my cynicism. "'This is not something in a million years I could have imagined having to do,' Mayor Bill de Blasio, appearing visibly distraught, said on Sunday (March 15th, 2020), adding that it was an 'extraordinarily painful' moment for the city schools. The closures will alter the lives and routines of 1.1 million children, 75,000 teachers and well over 1 million parents, and will no doubt prompt broader upheaval in a moment of profound anxiety for New Yorkers." (The New York Times, 2020).[1]

As Mayor de Blasio continued with his news briefing, I sat in front of my television like a deer in headlights. The shock of his words landed on my eardrums like a grenade thrown at rival soldiers engaged in a civil war. His words were not only shocking but also potent enough to render me deaf to all other sounds around me. He continued, stating that schools would be closed on the following Monday for all students and staff, but teachers would be asked to report to work later in the week for training on "remote learning." I pondered his words as if I were a contestant on the iconic game show *Jeopardy,* and using the clues included in the "Education in America" category, I answered my pondering self in true *Jeopardy* form: "What is remote learning?"

"By March 23, 2020, the city moved to fully remote learning and the system closed except for several dozen school buildings throughout the city, which would be used as learning centers to support the children of essential workers like health care workers." (The New York Times, 2020).[1] Again... in my *Jeopardy* state of mind, I offered my mental response: "What are learning centers?" What had just happened? In the blink of an eye, not the blink of a human eye but in what seemed like the blink of the eye of a diurnal bird basking in the sunlight, all that I had learned and come to know in my 26 years as an educator was obsolete. I was hearing jargon I was unfamiliar with. Where did the concept of remote learning come from? It seemed to me like it was dropped from outer space like a meteorite rapidly hurtling to the earth, leaving nothing in its path but disruption and destruction. In spite of this new reality, the remote learning concept was about to impact my world as an educator in an inconceivable way.

While pursuing my formal graduate education, I was afforded the opportunity to study and analyze a variety of leadership styles. Very early on in that journey, I self-identified as a cross between a transformational leader and a servant leader. Aligning with the attributes that informed both of these leadership styles, it was imperative that I pour into a hand-picked team both personally, professionally, and spiritually. This investment in the human spirit is what I cashed in on when I was faced with the challenge to lead a school in the midst of a pandemic. I often stated to my team, "Please indulge me because I do not know how to separate my thoughts on leadership from my belief system. My leadership style, my strong-willed personality, and my sense of dedication and commitment are all informed by my faith. I am cognizant of the physical space (a school) from which my leadership seat dwells, however, absent of my faith to guide my thoughts and actions, my leadership responses would present themselves very differently. Being also cognizant of the tenet of the separation of church and state, I concluded for myself that I am still not capable of leading effectively without acknowledging the impact my faith has on how I approach leadership. Josh Stephens states in his leadership and personal development blog, "Your faith (what you believe) is the cornerstone of your leadership style... and what you believe impacts how you lead." Using the Bible as my life guide, 2 Timothy 1:7 served as a precursor to fully understanding what it means to lead fearlessly. The Scripture tells us, "For God has not given us the spirit of fear, but of power, and love, and of a sound mind."

Fear is defined as "an unpleasant emotion caused by the belief that someone or something is dangerous and is likely to cause pain, or a threat."[2] The onset of the global coronavirus pandemic evoked fear of infection on a formidable level. The most obvious kind of fear was personal in nature. Fear for our individual and personal well-being was first and foremost on everyone's mind. However, a close second issue of concern was the impact of the pandemic on our professional livelihoods. This was no different for me in my capacity as an elementary school principal. The latter section of the anchor verse in 2 Timothy 1:7 rebukes the notion of succumbing to fear of any kind. The prevalence of fear in any situation negates the declaration Paul made to Timothy in reference to his leadership role at Ephesus. It is suggested that Timothy was content with his role serving alongside Paul and did not possess the characteristics of the outspoken leader of the huge Christian movement of their time.

Paul urged Timothy to stand strong and reminded him that God had bestowed upon him a spirit or attitude of power, love, and a sound mind. In keeping with the fidelity of the definition of fear, it is safe to say that fear is engendered from the lack of an attitude of power, love, and a sound mind. The fear of getting infected with the Coronavirus stemmed from a sense of a lack of power and a lack of a sound mind. The perception of a lack of love, a lack of power, or a lack of a sound mind will always result in a spirit of fear. Comprehending this biblical truth about fear enabled me to feel empowered to embrace the dictate that Paul declared over Timothy when he attempted to assist him with understanding what God says about leadership. According to the Bible, fear doesn't generate from God. In recalling the anchor verse in 2 Timothy, the verse says, "But God hath not given us a spirit of fear." In fact, it says He gives us the opposite—"but of power, and of love, and of a sound mind." If it doesn't come from God, then from where does fear generate? 1 Peter 5:8 tells us the enemy is our adversary who appears like a lion that roams around looking for whom he can devour and destroy. Anyone or anything that causes us to feel powerless or unloved, or causes our thinking to be distorted, is not of or from God. We are spiritual beings undergoing human experiences. The spirit that Paul speaks of is powerful and it is important that we acknowledge the power of "a spirit." Paul admonishes Timothy to not embrace a spirit of fear and reminds him that he was given a mighty spirit of power, love, and a sound mind.

When we live spirit-mindedly, even when we physically transition, it is believed that our spirit lives on. This mindfulness of the spirit being powerful enough to exist absent from the body speaks to the enduring power of the spirit we all possess.

However, because of the power we believe our God-assigned spirits possess and what we have come to know of what the human spirit is capable of enduring, when our spirit is broken or in a state of fear, it is easy to falsely rationalize that life as we have come to know it is over, that it has changed forever. The irony of this thinking is that life as we have come to know it, envision it, or even imagine it is indeed over. But God uses our shortcomings or perceived failures to bring us to a heightened level of spiritual awareness and resolve.

It has been in seasons of change, disruption, and strife that God has revealed Himself to me. Throughout my life, God has provided opportunities for me to prepare for "seasons of change," but I was busy doing me and doing life. Left to my own devices and exercising my God-conveyed free will, I was oblivious to the signs. I wasn't paying attention to the events which were unfolding around me as we transitioned into a pandemic state of emergency. Whenever we experience a challenge in the natural realm, God always provides a season of preparation, as well as a mode of escape in the spiritual realm. So how does one lead fearlessly in the midst of a global pandemic? The answer again is embedded in the Scriptures God left us with to guide our hearts, minds, and spirits. We must lead from a place of power, love, and a sound mind.

Subsequent to the mayor's announcement to close schools, many changes were introduced and implemented over a very brief transitional period. No sooner than I implemented one new policy, a hybrid of the original new policy was being introduced. It was and continues to be a very frustrating state of affairs. Principals are expected to oversee rigorous instruction for all students in spite of a new policy which would allow teachers and support staff to acquire medical accommodations to work remotely. This new policy resulted in a tremendously reduced number of teachers and support staff in school buildings. Needless to say, this scenario was just one of the many challenges that rendered me feeling powerless. This clashing of pedagogical and personnel policies prompted the spirit of fear to rise up in me as it relates to power. I felt powerless over a situation that I perceived I had no control over but was being told I was responsible to oversee within the leadership framework dictated by the New York City Department of Education.

In my *Jeopardy* voice deep in my spirit, I posed the question in true *Jeopardy* fashion, "How do you lead fearlessly when you feel powerless?" The Bible says God gives us a spirit of power. When Paul wrote to Timothy, a young Christian leader at the time, Christians throughout the world were being crucified. The situation for Christians, God's people, couldn't have been more dire than it was at that time, so who was I to feel powerless and fearful? I cashed in on all the conversations of encouragement, guidance, and empowerment that I had provided for my team and I put all trust in God thereby reclaiming my God-appointed power over that situation. In essence, I chose to lead with power.

As I struggled with leading fearlessly, again I meditated on the anchor Scripture and contemplated the thought, *Why would God allow something like this to occur?* Does He not have all things in His hands? Does God not love His people? So, in *Jeopardy* fashion, I posed yet another question to myself, "What does God's love feel like?" In exploring the Scriptures, Romans 5:12 reminded me that mankind opened the portal that allowed sin to enter into the world and it's that same sin that causes death. God is not the author of any manner of chaos, but we are assured that even in the midst of chaos "All things work for good to those who love God, to those who are called according to His purpose." Simultaneously, He promised to never leave us nor forsake us. So, in the midst of the pandemic, I divvied up affirmations, confirmations, and an abundance of "Thank you" and "I appreciate you" declarations. I chose to stand steadfast on these two truths: All things work for good to those who love God and are called according to His purpose and God will never leave us or forsake us. God has proven over and over again that He loves me. For that reason, I chose to lead from a place of love.

Continuing on this journey of leading in the midst of a pandemic, I resorted to a statement I have repeated many hundreds of times over the course of my fourteen-year tenure as a principal. Whenever I needed to make a leadership decision of which the responsibility of the outcome fell solely on my shoulders and in my lap, I would loudly proclaim: "I do things that make sense!" If what I implemented or directed someone to do turned out to be a bad decision, I regrouped and incorporated the outcome into a life lesson or teachable moment. I was content with the outcome because I had chosen to lead with a sound mind in consultation with the Father.

So, we've come to my final *Jeopardy* question. "What does it look like to lead fearlessly?" Leading fearlessly means leading with the knowledge that God has bestowed a power upon us that no man or woman can upstage. It further means, it doesn't matter what your title is because God doesn't honor or recognize titles. He honors and recognizes a servant's heart for His people. Secondly, leading fearlessly means being a living, transparent, and available example of God's love for His people. I would bet money that most non-believers do not read the Bible, so their "bible" is represented by those in their midst who proclaim to be walking the Christian path. They can only see the love of God through our interactions with them. Moments of leadership interactions are a prime way to display what God's love for His people looks like through acts of compassion, understanding, and acceptance. Lastly, leading fearlessly is exhibited by being thoughtful, purposeful, and intentional about our leadership.

My school logo includes a foundational base with three pillars. The base is represented by the word believe. And upon the belief base stands the pillars of which the words purpose, intention, and motivation are represented. In all that I attempt to navigate in leadership, as well as in life, I ask myself three questions before engaging in what I deem difficult or challenging conversations:

- What is my motivation? (Why am I having this conversation?)

- What is my purpose? (Do I want to resolve something or convey information?)

- What is my intention? (What is the intended outcome of this conversation?)

Through this self-check, I am engaging in actions to lead with a sound mind. I model this personally with my family and professionally with my leadership team. I choose to lead with a sound mind. In a nutshell, leading fearlessly occurs when we allow God into the mix to provide the supernatural increase we need to influence others through a clear display of His bestowed power, unwavering love, and sound mindedness.

Sources: 1. Shapiro, E. (2020). The New York Times. *New York City Public Schools to Close to Slow Spread of Coronavirus.* www.nytimes.com; 2. Oxford Languages (2021)

You Can't Control the Wind, but You Can Learn How to Fly

Diannah "Brooklyn" Sparks

I was forced to leave my dream job as a flight attendant a little over two years after becoming a mother. I eventually found another career path in the airline industry. This time underneath airplanes as a ramp agent and baggage handler. It was a different world to say the least. A lot less glamorous, and a whole lot more physically demanding. Imagine crawling into and out of airplane cargo holds and loading and unloading luggage, mail, packages, and over ten thousand pounds of cargo from an aircraft... being a 5'3" woman... on a tight timeline... outside, in the winter, aka cold and freezing temperatures, snow, sleet, hail (holiday season at that)... mostly on heavy-loaded international flights. And if you're originally from another country outside of the US (especially my people from the Caribbean, Latin America, Africa, etc.), you KNOW you can't fly "back home" without maximizing every bag and pound of your luggage allowance and shipping a loaded barrel or two! Now picture your loaded barrels and all your bags times more than 100 for each passenger on each flight.

The caveat is this: I was pregnant with my second child, and I WORKED all the way through to the end of my pregnancy. I never took maternity leave, and I actually ended up going into labor on my day off! (Don't judge me!) I should add here that I was also hit by a car one day while crossing the street during that pregnancy. It knocked the wind out of me and flipped me into the air before my body slammed onto the pavement. No broken bones, but I did suffer injuries that made it difficult to return to my position on the ramp after my maternity leave ended. I remained on leave with the company for two years, 2018 to 2020, as I waited for other positions to become available.

I know it sounds cliché, but I knew 2020 would be a year like no other. On New Year's Day, while in another city, I got a call from back home that we lost a childhood friend to suicide (I lost a second friend to suicide two months later, just prior to the pandemic). It was completely unexpected and devastating. I was asked to come back to the block we grew up on and pray at a vigil held in his honor. I felt numb and confused. What could I say? I tried to write some notes down, but nothing came to me. I completely blanked out. As they called my name to come up, I mumbled a quick prayer to God asking that my words would bring comfort, peace, healing, and hope. I got to the front and looked up at the sea of faces, most of them familiar faces I recognized from childhood and a few I couldn't quite place, but the commonality was the overwhelming feeling of hurt, shock, confusion, some anger, and sorrow. I took a deep breath, closed my eyes, and began to speak: "None of us knew this would happen. We can't control everything that happens TO us, but we CAN control how we respond to these things. Let's allow this to change us for the better."

I've seen so many plans fade away or completely destroyed because of just one loss, one death, one tragedy, or one crisis. We've all experienced this in one way or another, and most likely long before 2020. Tragedy forces us to think of what we could've, should've, or would've done differently with the time we used to have before it struck. That's why I'm not big on New Year's resolutions. There's absolutely nothing wrong with them, I just don't think that I should wait for a new year to make necessary changes or act on my plans. I believe that change can and should come at any time, as soon as possible. I was tempted to join in the cries of "Man, this year is messed up already," but I decided then and there to allow that tragedy to be a catalyst for triumph instead of saying it ruined my year. I was focused and determined, both in my personal and professional life. I set short and long-term goals for each. I created a vision board AND wrote out my vision and goals so that I could constantly see and speak what I was believing for and working toward.

Just a few days after the vigil, almost two years to the date when I first took a leave of absence, I finally got the call for a new position with my airline. I was to report to work at five in the morning the following Monday. I take public transportation to work, so that means I had to leave home by three in the morning to take the train and then the bus and the AirTran to make sure that I made it there on time. That also meant I needed to wake up to get dressed and start my day at 2:00 a.m. or maybe even earlier, which also meant I should probably get everything my toddler-aged daughters needed for their day prepared the night before (hair done, clothes out, lunches packed, etc.), and try to be in bed by 9:00 p.m. to make sure I had enough rest to be functional on the job. Never in my life have I gone to bed by 9:00 p.m. I had no idea how I was going to make it work, but I made the necessary sacrifices and changes, networked with my family and support system to make it happen.

I was excited to get back into the swing of things at the airport. I missed the hustle and bustle of the airport—walking through the terminal hearing flight announcements, looking at the cities on the departure and arrivals board while planning and daydreaming about my next travel adventure, meeting and talking to passengers about their travels, and then seeing them off or welcoming them to their destinations. Things were looking up. My airline was thriving. Our airport was selected as the Hub of the Year for outstanding performance and commitment to customers, customer service, and safety. The company even commissioned a custom designed airplane that featured a giant THANK YOU written across the body of the aircraft. Stenciled inside the enormous letters on each side are the names of each employee, worldwide. After 10 years in the industry, I felt proud to be recognized and included in this token of appreciation. The year 2020 was looking up.

Then came the month of March. The airport had already been abuzz with talk and rumors about the new strain of Coronavirus for a few weeks, but on March 1, the first confirmed case of COVID-19 was documented in New York City. Day by day, case by case, memo by memo, flight by flight, I saw the decline from what was once a bustling airport to a place that was nearly a ghost town. Planes were flying nearly empty. Eventually, 90 percent of the flights were canceled. What remained was just a handful of passengers on a handful of flights whose prices had been dropped so low they were almost giving tickets away. Then halfway through the month, as cases began to soar and New York City was declared the epicenter of the pandemic, all the schools and child care facilities were closed indefinitely. All my careful planning was out the window. I knew I couldn't continue working without consistent child care and with my support system on quarantine. Every day became a "wake up and see what happens" kind of day. As an essential worker, it was already both challenging and frightening to continue working while being concerned for my own health and safety; meanwhile, family and friends began to lose loved ones to COVID-19 on a daily basis.

By the end of March, I was once again out of work, unsure of what was to come. March came in like a lion, but it definitely did not go out like a lamb! As the summer months approached, I realized that my uncertainty for what I thought would be just "the next few weeks" would extend well into the next several months, and quite possibly, the next few years. As was forecasted back in March 2020 when everything first began to shut down, the Coronavirus pandemic had devastated the aviation industry. Most airlines had to lay off a significant portion of their workforce. A lot of my colleagues were forced into early retirement. The school boards in my city still (in my opinion) had not figured out the safest and most feasible way to reopen schools for the fall. I couldn't return to work if I wanted to.

Grace periods, assistance programs, and moratoriums were lapsing. On top of all that, I was mentally and emotionally weary from the constant fight against racism and injustice, intensified by the senseless deaths of people like Breonna Taylor, Ahmaud Arbery, and George Floyd. On top of that, it was disheartening to see the increasing crime in the city that came with the warmer weather months. It was all becoming too much. I had to unplug and take a break from the news and social media. I longed for the carefree pre-pandemic days. I became numb to the present and began to look to the long-gone past and the far-off future for the solutions as I took each passing day for granted.

I was slowly losing the excitement and optimism I held a few months prior. Instead of speaking and declaring blessings and life, I began to curse the gift of a passing year by saying things like "This year is trash" and "Soon as this year is over, I'm going to _____." We can get so caught up in what we want to do or what we used to do that we miss the chance to fully experience and appreciate what we CAN do or what is happening right now.

One day, on "Throwback Thursday" (a new tradition I made up during the pandemic where I would watch old movies or TV shows), I watched the classic Eddie Murphy comedy *Coming to America*. The main character, Prince Akeem, haphazardly decides to leave his wealth and beautiful kingdom in Africa and travel to America in search of true love. He lands in the hood, in Queens... I mean THE HOOD... 1980's slums Queens! Abandoned buildings, rats, drug addicts, hustlers, con artists, and Jeri curls. Everything around him was trashed. He was in what most people would consider a horrible place, but he was so excited about the here and now that he didn't even notice, or at least he didn't let it discourage him. He was robbed, cursed out, taken advantage of, and placed in dangerous and unfavorable situations throughout the movie, but his demeanor remained the same: excited, willing to learn, and hopeful. Perspective is everything. A glass of water can be seen as half empty or half full depending on how you choose to view it.

I live in a high-rise apartment building. I can see the local hospital from my window. My neighbors down the hall can also see the hospital, but the view they have isn't the same as mine because they're seeing a different side of the hospital. The same can be said of my neighbors who live on higher or lower floors. If I go outside, I can see the hospital, too. But my view won't be the same as it was looking out of my window. The same can be said for those inside of the hospital. All those different vantage points, but the hospital remains the same. It hasn't moved or changed one bit, yet it looks completely different in each scenario. The only thing that has changed is how it's viewed. The same can be said of the pandemic.

I lost a lot, but I gained so much more. I didn't make a million dollars. I didn't invest in stocks or Bitcoin (yet). I didn't get a celebrity endorsement or shout out, and I didn't go viral on social media. Yeah, I "lost time," but I redefined and created so much more time. I did get to refocus and rest. I did get to spend time taking care of me. I did get to focus on my children and family. I did get to finish books that I started reading. I did get to reexplore and fall in love with my neighborhood and city again. I did get to spend time volunteering with organizations making a difference in the community. I did get to participate in and lead protests across the city (and even in Washington, DC). I did get to demand justice and be an ally and voice for the oppressed and the disadvantaged. I did get to give time and resources to people in need. I did my best to support every business owner and small business that I know. I got to sleep past 7:00 a.m. I got to homeschool my children (which is something I've always wanted to do), and teach them firsthand what it means to unite and stand up for what you believe in and for what is right. Whether it was explaining why we need to wear masks, or why the white refrigerated trucks were outside of the hospital that we could see from our windows, or opening those same windows every evening at 7:00 p.m. to make noise, clap, whistle, and bang pots and bottles and toy instruments as a way of saying thank you to the healthcare and essential workers keeping our city and world going.

I did get to spend more time with God, not just asking for what I want, but listening to His heart and being still enough to really know and understand that He is good. I did get to pray, fervently, like my grandmother used to. I discovered new brands, businesses, foods, places, and more. I took free courses online with Ivy League schools. I attended workshops and conferences that I wouldn't have been able to afford the year prior. I found new mentors, and new people to network and build with. I started the nail polish line that my daughter has been asking for since she was two. I have purposed to take advantage of every window of opportunity that the pandemic has opened, instead of staring and fussing at the doors that it has closed. I made a conscious and deliberate decision to move from survival mode to thriving mode.

We tend to live life in anticipation of the next thing, place, achievement, day off, etc., instead of making the most of each day and moment we are in. We can't always choose what things will impact us, but we CAN control HOW they affect us. You CAN learn to fly. Don't let the "wind" of the COVID-19 pandemic cancel your life's flight. Adjust your wings, brace yourself, and keep flying.

B-I-S-H, Now What You Gonna Do?

Tanisha Gaskin-Christie

Some people say the f word, others say OMG. Me, I have a whole phrase and internal pep talk. When things go wrong or when there is an unexpected "not today devil because I don't need another thing to add to my already full life," I have a whole turn to camera left moment and ask myself, "B-I-S-H, now what you gonna do?" I never answer myself back though. As my grandmother would say, "You can talk to yourself all you want just as long as you don't answer yourself back because then you're crazy."

In a womb talk (a sacred gut to heart conversation without judgment and boundaries) with my cousin's wife, she asked me that question and the phrase ignited an inner switch that illuminated the issue at hand that I needed to solve. Since then, it's the question that I ask myself when faced with adversity.

Asking myself that question allows me to compartmentalize my thoughts and emotions when I need to handle unexpected events. I don't want anyone to think that I just blurt out curse words for naught but honestly, the B-I-S-H is my sequence of dismantling emotions from the onset of an unexpected crisis and moving into a strategic mindset to tackle what's at hand. So of course, when the news channels started to broadcast in early March that there's this unknown virus and the word pandemic started to become real, I turned left and blurted out my "B-I-S-H," then I went into survival mode.

The day my office announced that we would all be working remotely starting the next day was March 17, 2020. By that time, all news channels were beginning to provide more details on the newly discovered COVID-19. On one of the news shows, I can't remember if it was CNN or NBC, they started to post the segment of the population most likely to get the virus. I had another turn to the left camera moment when I heard: "Diabetes... overweight." I have to admit that hearing those two things gave me a moment of clarity. Granted, I have definitely had my fair share of adversity, tragedy, and grief, but the pandemic caused me to take a realistic view of my health and how it could impact everyone around me. For the first time, my health became more than my own problem. In my eyes, it became a means to my family's survival. B-I-S-H, since COVID, has become an autopilot response to navigating through personal and business responsibilities by helping me organize my thoughts and develop a pivot to an obstacle at hand.

B stands for brutal honesty. When faced with an unexpected crisis, denial is not in anyone's best interest. My fight was in high gear, especially during the pandemic, so I had to speak truth to myself. You see, my health according to the CDC was putting me at greater risk for becoming infected. Being plus-size and prediabetic were two things that I didn't take seriously until the pandemic. I had to be brutally honest with myself once I realized that as a mom with a fit, essential-worker husband and three amazing boys, I was the weakest link in the chain. I also knew that I was the backbone of my family and they all draw strength from me. Being transparent with myself allowed me to see things as they are, period. Although confident and plus-size, my pudgy cakes put me at a greater risk of possibly not surviving COVID-19 if I contracted the virus, which would put my family at risk. I needed to change that. This was the truth. Brutal honesty helps you to uncover the issue as it is so that you can then identify what resources you have or don't have in order to address the issue at hand.

My other b-word is basic. Getting down to the basics, the nitty-gritty of the issue, is essential for pivoting during a crisis. During this new norm of

COVID-19, there isn't time to romanticize or complicate the issues that need my immediate attention. My basics were simple. My family and I needed to be healthy and safe in order for us to survive and thrive and I needed to preserve myself because I am the strongest in my family. Many times when we are faced with adversity, we start to let our emotions outweigh our logic. When that happens, we can lose the precious time needed to really nip the problem in the bud. The pandemic forced me to put my health first and to clearly communicate my needs to my family. That was a huge part of building the foundation for creating a plan of action to keep us safe. But I also needed to take the time to make sure that I was well—emotionally, physically, and financially. The Christie's COVID-19 Family Plan was simple: limit my outside exposure (i.e., my husband would take on the grocery shopping) and increase my sacred time for wellness.

I stand for instincts. My childhood forced me to grow up very quickly. Let's just say that the environment that I grew up in was fast-paced. After losing my parents in my teens, I learned very early on to trust my instincts because, as an only child, they were all I had. Your instincts, in my opinion, are little whispers from God that give direction and do not lie. Being fully self-aware and transparent helps you to develop heightened discernment.

My other i-word is implement. The Christie's COVID-19 Family Plan would have been just a thought without implementing it. My inner fight response kicked in big time and we moved as a unit to keep everyone healthy and to address my personal weight issues. It's funny to think of what will make you move when your back is against the wall. I'm glad that I chose to not only think about my next best steps but to actually take the steps. I don't believe in sitting in dung. I'm a visual person. Imagine sitting there in a pile of pooh doing nothing. For me, there's no choice but to take action. Implementation is crucial to see what will play out. I devised a plan of action and implemented it. Needless to say, I am down eighteen pounds and up $10k in my cash cushion. My husband can spot a sale at the grocery store like nobody's business and our three sons recycle, do laundry, and wash dishes without being asked. This would be the perfect place for a cheesing emoji. The pandemic showed my family and I that actions matter. So, implementing steps to help make our well-being better only led to a better condition for us all.

S stands for self-care. The stress that kicks in when faced with a crisis can be detrimental to one's emotional and mental well-being. In the New York Times article, "The Strong and Stressed Black Woman," Dr. Burnett-Zeigler wrote: "Black women are more likely than white women to have experienced post-traumatic stress disorder resulting from childhood maltreatment and sexual and physical violence. They are more likely to have stress related to family, employment, finances, discrimination or racism and safety concerns associated with living in high crime neighborhoods."

Self-care is essential and more so when faced with a crisis. Oftentimes, for far too many, self-care is the last thing on the list or it is not on the list at all. But during the pandemic, self-care was essential for me to have the tools necessary to break down the issue, implement my plan to fix it, and to be whole at the end of the day. There was a time when I felt quite guilty about putting my own needs first, but I realized that by putting my own needs at the forefront I became able to give myself more fully to things and people that matter most in my life. Self-care was also something that I implemented in my business. You see, I am a leader in a direct sales company where I have the huge honor of supporting over 100 women on their journey to financial stability. Self-care was now my norm and as I gradually made myself a priority, I realized how it impacted all areas of my life. It also became a common topic of conversation in my circle of influence. For instance, out of my desire to fit physical activity into my week, I implemented group Zoom sessions for others to join. To my surprise, the feedback received was that the activity was needed and should be continued. Thus, Zumba Happy Hour was birthed. We all agreed to put self-care first. In doing so, we implemented things in our businesses that would not have taken off or taken place otherwise.

My other s-word is speak up. Picture me in the Spike Lee movie *School Daze* saying this to you and myself. Can I get a bull horn? Speaking up saved my sanity and allowed me to implement changes that have improved my health. I am guilty of being the do-it-all-I-got-it person, but the pandemic taught me how to speak up because there wasn't any time to waste with me trying to do it all myself. NOT AT ALL. I didn't need to mince words with what I needed, who I needed help from, how they were to help, etc. My health needed to be snatched; I needed wholeness so that I could perform my best for my family. I honestly feel that some of my hardest moments were when I bottled up everything and tried to figure out things myself. I am so grateful that I overcame that.

My third s-word is stash. Whether in a cushion, a safe, under the bed, or in the closet, a stash of cash (especially in a pandemic) matters. Having an emergency savings fund in cash became essential for my husband and me as a result of the pandemic. I realized the first couple of days after the shutdown that cash on hand would be necessary. I remember on 9/11 when the towers fell, I ran into a shoe store to get sneakers and the registers were down. Luckily I had $40 in cash on me, but a few others did not and had to either run barefoot or in heels. That image has stuck with me. So, having at least $10,000 in cash in my stash became part of our plan of action. The lack of financial resources in a crisis can affect how you approach developing a plan to overcome what you're facing at the present time. I believe that financial stability provides choices. By opening my mouth to the women in my business, I realized this was a truth that we all shared. So, we committed to putting ourselves as well as our financial needs first. I have to say that it is an absolute blessing to be able to go to the grocery store without having to go to the ATM. And for a family of five with four males, the grocery bill is huge.

H stands for honoring signature relationships. The key relationships that you form are essential in all aspects of your life, but they are spotlighted and sometimes tested in times of crisis. In my opinion, you honestly do not have time to bark up the wrong resource when you got to survive. Understanding signature relationships and honoring them is golden, especially if you need to draw from them. You honestly know who your friends are and who's going to stick by you when you are in need. The pandemic forced us to scrutinize our relationships with family, friends, institutions, and so on. Honoring my interaction with my bank, healthcare providers, children's teachers, job, business partners, customers, church, and community gave me a sense of security and empowerment. Had it not been for solid relationships, particularly with my instructor from the gym, I would have had no clue about the low-cost virtual fitness outlets that were just a click away. My gym instructor was also instrumental in helping me host the fitness event for others which reinforced how essential our health is. The relationships with friends who knew of my necessities varied at times. Whether it was disinfectant, tissue, or if they were at BJs stocking up and texted to see if I needed anything, their support helped tremendously as we weathered the storm.

But the most important and honored relationship that tops it all for me and my family is with God. Faith is essential; it keeps my family and I grounded. Our faith helps us honor the abundance of people God has placed in our lives for a reason, a season, and also a lifetime.

So, you see, B-I-S-H is my tried-and-true way of snapping myself into reality and igniting my fight or flight mode so that I can understand the basics of what's taking place in my life. It is my way of honing my instincts so that I can implement the right and the best solution for what has been put in front of me. It is also my reminder to put self-care first so that I do not succumb to stressors when I speak up. It is my driving force for securing my stash to ensure that I can financially address issues that may arise, resulting in peace of mind. It is honoring my faith and being grateful for those key relationships that I can deposit into and draw from when I am faced with weathering an unexpected crisis.

2020 in Perspective

Oluwatoyin Ayanfodun

"Tough times don't last, tough people do."
—Unknown

Ding, ding, ding! "As we prepare for landing, please check that your seatbelts are fastened, seats and tray tables are up, and your electronics are in airplane mode or off," she said chipperly as we started the process of preparing to land at LaGuardia Airport in New York City. Ding, ding, ding! The lights came on, the front doors opened, and yup, just like that we had landed safely. Another amazing vacation trip accomplished!

From sunny beaches to clear skies, and yes, some turbulence here and there, I can be transparent and say that the daydreams of my last major vacation in November 2019 rang in my mind and heart throughout 2020. Yet, I can be even more transparent and say that the work that ensued right after the sparkly ball dropped in Times Square showed me that resilience is a force that is built within throughout all of life's struggles. The year 2020 was a reality check.

"You can only become truly accomplished at something you love. Don't make money your goal. Instead pursue the things you love doing and then do them so well that people can't take their eyes off of you."

—Maya Angelou

Growing up in the 90's as a young male in Brooklyn, New York, had its ups and downs, as growing up anywhere may have. During my senior year in high school, I became truly inspired by the power of education, educators, mentors, and coaches.

But before I continue, let me quickly introduce myself! My name is Oluwatoyin Ayanfodun. Most of my peers and colleagues lovingly call me Toyin. I am a social entrepreneur who has dedicated my life to the call of helping at-risk youth and families overcome social, emotional, and academic challenges. As a proud Nigerian born and raised in Brooklyn, tough times came and went. Yet, one thing always rang true—I saw people I love fighting for the things they believed in. Their fight and watching young people in my community who were underrepresented and underserved was the beginning of a life of service that drove me to start Tomorrow's Leaders NYC (TLNYC), a nine-year-old 501(c)(3) nonprofit organization that offers support services in the Bronx and Brooklyn.

"Belief in oneself and knowing who you are, I mean, that's the foundation for everything great."

—Jay-Z

The faith that I have in life is real. The feeling that I get when I know something can or will work in a young person's life is real. Being able to mentor and coach the students of today into the leaders of tomorrow is real. And yes, the obstacles that 2020 presented were also extremely real!

So, let's get right to it. The year 2020 showed up and packed a punch that I never thought I would see. From opening the year with layoffs and no school partnerships to producing a basketball tournament on a shoestring budget while working to figure out how the organization would stay afloat, the light that lives inside of me felt like it wanted to dwindle. Natural right? I believe so. However, the obstacles only got bigger.

From losing over $100,000 in funding, to watching the pandemic wreak havoc on the support services that help the communities I serve, to then having to say goodbye to one of my closest friends due to gun violence, issue after issue worked to dim my never-ending battery of joy. Then, enter the spirit of self-doubt! *Is it me?* I asked myself. *Am I still the person for this?* my mind wondered over and over again. *Is it possible to turn this around?* My mind swirled with questions, many of which I had no immediate answers to. I knew what had to be done. I felt it. It was right in front of me. "What was it?" you may ask. I had to keep moving. Move beyond the fear. Move beyond the issues. Find ways to pivot with power while keeping the organization afloat.

With less than $2 in the company bank account, which resulted in layoffs followed by an abrupt resignation, I can honestly say I was scared. Not scared for myself but scared for those in my care. Those who had been forgotten, but I pledged to always see them. And yes, those who I had to let go from employment.

"I have learned over the years that when one's mind is made up, this diminishes fear; knowing what must be done does away with fear."

—Rosa Parks

Created long ago, the core values of Tomorrow's Leaders started to ring and repeat loudly in my psyche daily. Transparency. Authentic relationship. Persistence. Consistency. Support system. Patience. Were those words in the story of how the organization would bounce back? What did those words have to do with the struggles we were seeing and facing? How could they help us restart the momentum that continued to fluctuate due to a variety of issues including the pandemic? Well, those questions were answered and funding resurfaced as I started to do one thing that many have said I should do more of—self-care.

"Yes we can!"

—Barack Obama

For some, 2020 may have seemed gloomy and full of despair. For others, 2020 may have been the year they never asked for. For me, 2020 was the year that reminded me that managing the trying times while taking in each lesson is tremendously important. The year 2020 reminded me that self-care is not selfish as I cannot be of assistance to others if I am personally depleted. It reminded me that alongside my love of community, I also had to continue to love and honor myself through days off and professional development. Your days are yours. Take them when needed. The year 2020 also reminded me of the importance of my authentic relationships within my support system. A system that honors transparent conversations and values my individual uniqueness and needs. It was also the year that reminded me that something being imperfect does not mean that it is invalid or invaluable. In 2020, I was also reminded that perfection is not real and it's okay to be transparent with those close and not so close to you. I was reminded that I can have a personal life while managing a professional life which then equates to me being optimistic about my short and long-term personal and professional goals. Most of all, 2020 was the year that reminded me that networking is vital to the success of any organization. Yes, the work you do is essential; however, functioning in a silo is dangerous to the overall well-being of your organization.

"Not everything that is faced can be changed.
But nothing can be changed until it is faced."

—James Baldwin

The Power of the Pivot

Tash Leath-Hamilton

I am an intuitive life coach. I have the innate ability to see a person's past, present, and future. When I was six years old, God blessed me with this gift—and I knew I wanted to use it to help people. As an intuitive guru, I am able to help people by sensing what they have experienced along with what lies ahead. I use this gift of intuition, or foresight, to help people shift their mindset, change their behaviors, and create their best life.

It is safe to say that 2020 taught us a lot of lessons: Be grateful for the things in your life that really matter like family and friends. Self-care is of the utmost importance. Rethink the 9-to-5 structure and overall American work culture. Creativity will take us far. Appreciate what you have because things could always be way worse.

I have provided services to all sorts of people—celebrities, international business owners, and even Fortune 500 companies. I do the work that I do to better people's lives. I recognize that the potential for greatness lies in each and every one of us. We just need to tap into it. Through my line of work in 2020, I knew the struggles many of my clients were experiencing and how they could overcome them. However, many of them did not discover their struggles or successes until they were forced to sit still.

It saddened me to see so many people lost and not cognizant of their struggles until 2020 forced them to take a hard look in the mirror. I knew that I needed to go in another direction when I saw so many of them hurting. From coaching them, I knew the problems they faced, but many were either oblivious or in denial until the pandemic. When the country was locked down, many of them had no other choice but to come to grips with their issues. They then reached out to me.

I asked myself, *How can I help? What can I do to make their lives better? What is within my power to change?* Their struggles challenged me to be more of a servant-leader and look within for additional ways I can serve my community through the work that I do. I expanded my business model and started offering additional services to accommodate as many people as possible. Overall, I increased their access to me.

My clients faced many hardships in 2020, as did millions of people across the globe. Here are some examples of the crises a few of them faced during the COVID-19 pandemic and how I was able to help them overcome their struggles during such a difficult time. I hope that you use these stories to motivate you and show you that if they can overcome these adversities, you can too.

- Client #1 is a warehouse manager for a small, family-owned courier company in Metro Atlanta, and his company was hit hard by the pandemic. He explained to me that he ran the company's shipping and receiving ventures and supervised five company truck drivers. Initially, upon receiving news that operations were going to be reduced by 50 percent, it alarmed him tremendously. His first thoughts were that he was going to have to lay off at least half of his drivers and that he would be limited to handling all of the day-to-day operations within the warehouse himself. But before he could even begin to investigate the magnitude of the situation, he arrived at work one day and the doors were padlocked. His employees were waiting on him with looks of sheer concern and fear about the future for themselves and their families.

Their lives had been changed in an instant, which was the beginning of some of the most difficult financial times that he had ever faced in his life. Client #1 explained to me that he was a newlywed that had just purchased a new home and truck within the past six months and, out of nowhere, he was having to try and figure out how to survive on unemployment, which was not even a fraction of his yearly salary. For months he had to survive on a hope and a prayer that his company would reopen or that the pandemic would leave as fast as it came. Neither happened, and tensions within his home were at an all-time high.

I encouraged Client #1 to apply for unemployment and all the programs offered by local and federal agencies to assist formerly employed individuals affected by the crisis. I also urged him to have faith in what he prayed for and to be patient enough to trust the process. After several weeks of waiting, he was finally accepted into the programs he had applied for, which enabled him to regain his financial stability and move forward with his life.

Takeaway #1: In times of crisis, have faith, patience, and trust the process.

- Client #2 is a single mother of three from Baltimore. She was forced to work only 20 hours per week due to her company cutting hours. As a customer service representative at a telemarketing company, her industry was one of the first to be negatively affected by social distancing mandates in the beginning stages of COVID-19. She was not able to afford her apartment after her hours were cut, and it led to Client #2 and her children facing eviction during one of the scariest and most uncertain times in US history.

I was introduced to Client #2 through a mutual acquaintance, and I discussed with her the rental assistance program and eviction moratorium orders that had been imposed. I also encouraged her to regroup and refocus her energy into ensuring that she and her family were able to stay in their home. The information I provided allowed Client #2 and her family to not only save their home, but they were also able to receive the help they needed in all aspects of their lives, which had been altered in a way that would have ended up catastrophic in most cases.

Takeaway #2: In times of crisis, regroup and refocus your energy.

- Client #3 is an actress in Los Angeles who found herself going into a deep depression due to the pandemic. It affected every aspect of her life. She stopped eating, she stopped going outside, and she stepped back from her career. She watched her family, friends, and community get sick from COVID-19 and hundreds of thousands of Americans perish due to the disease. She stopped living and started existing.

I coached Client #3 through her personal crisis by encouraging her to look at the bigger picture and find her joy in the midst of the storm. I also encouraged her to look within to find her true self. Those tactics made Client #3 take that hard look in the mirror that, at some point in our lives, we all have to take. She was at a crossroads. Would she take the first path and lose herself forever, or would she take the second path and continue to be who she was destined to be? I am happy to report that she chose the latter.

Takeaway #3: In times of crisis, look at the big picture and find joy in the midst of the storm.

The stories of these clients represent t1he stories of millions of Americans. Many lost their homes and jobs and experienced depression and other ailments directly related to the pandemic. An unconscionable amount of people passed away. On a global level, the COVID-19 pandemic wreaked widespread havoc and forced us all to stand still.

So how do you move forward in crisis? How do you will yourself past the issues you are facing? How do you rise above? You pivot. Here are 10 tips to help you shift in your time of crisis for a successful outcome.

1. **Have faith.** You must always remember that everything will eventually work out. Do the work to ensure that it does, but also actually believe that it will. That will go a long way. Speak life over your situation and practice positivity. In every situation you face, boldly claim your affirmative outcome.

2. **Have patience.** When times get rough, you must know that you will get through it. You may not get immediate relief, but it will come eventually. As the saying goes, patience is a virtue. Practicing patience will benefit you greatly in the long run.

3. **Trust the process.** Sometimes the path to the other side of your breakthrough is dim. It may make you uncomfortable, but it is necessary. Just as a caterpillar becomes a butterfly, many times the process is not glamorous. It is meant

to mold you and make you beautiful. You must experience the rain to appreciate the sunshine.

4. **Regroup.** You may have to go back to the drawing board to get the results that you want. In crises, it may take rearranging your thoughts and actions to make it through. Know that reorganizing your strategy and how you will move forward does not diminish your journey nor your final destination.

5. **Refocus your energy.** Sometimes we focus on the wrong things during a crisis, such as "Why me?" or "How did this happen?" We get so caught up in the fact that the bad situation happened that all of our energy goes to the wrong thing. Instead, we should immediately ask ourselves how to move forward. Every bit of energy that we have for the matter should be diverted to the solution, not the problem.

6. **Remember to look at the big picture.** Society conditions us to look at the right now and small picture when it comes to our personal lives, such as our jobs, relationships, and housing, etc. Yet, oftentimes when we focus on the small picture, we miss the big picture. With each situation we face, we have to take a step back and look at the big picture. On a larger scale, what is this event connected to? Is there something greater to be learned from this incident?

7. **Find joy in the midst of the storm.** Have you ever had something good come out of a terrible situation? When the situation happened, you thought it was the end of the world. However, as time progressed, you realized that you benefited from that bad thing happening to you. When facing crises, we must remember that they exist to teach us lessons. Even if it seems impossible, find the good in adversity. You will respond more favorably to it and it will not be able to negatively affect you as much.

8. **Connect with others.** We sometimes devalue the importance of connecting with others. Many of us exist in our own little bubble in our own world and tune others out. A life without human connection can get lonely and cold. Be sure to make connecting with family and friends a priority. Fellowship is good for the soul.

9. **Breathe and meditate.** In crises, our first response is usually to react. However, before we act, we should take a deep breath and get centered. This allows us to act from a place of wisdom instead of emotion. Breathing and meditating first forces us to really think about the situation before we take another step. It enables us to make more rational decisions.

10. **Focus on what is within your control.** We spend a lot of time worrying about things we cannot control. That is human nature. However, I encourage you to focus on the things within your control to preserve your energy for what you can actually change. If all of your energy is used on problems you cannot control, by the time you face the issues you have the power to change, there is little you can do about them.

I hope these tips help you to utilize your power. Being flexible in the face of adversity can diminish the impact of negative situations and enable you to come out of them unscathed. It can also allow you to be able to adapt to change quickly and efficiently. There is power in being able to do this.

Ultimately, I was able to help hundreds of people get the truth and clarity they needed during the pandemic. Many people were dealt terrible blows in 2020. However, giving up was never an option. It is much easier to throw in the towel than it is to stay and fight. Being able to adapt to bad situations makes the fight much easier. Helping others get through the pandemic taught me a life lesson about the power of the pivot. Many times, if life gets us down, we stay stuck for a while. But we must always be willing to MOVE—sometimes to get out of our own way.

Pivot Your Mindset: Finding Healing, Strength, and Growth in a Time of Loss and Change

Sue Fearless

Where do I begin? I kept turning on the TV and the cases kept rising, the deaths kept rising, the uncertainty kept rising, and the truth was setting in that this was REAL. And then the city shut down and 2020 went dark. There we were... mandated to be home... trying to get last minute supplies... trying to comprehend what was going on. What would happen to our jobs? What would happen with our schools? How would we pay our bills? How would we provide our services? What would we do? A lot of us were feeling defeated.

I learned right away that the lesson was to take care of your health, make sure your business and your finances are in order, make sure you have enough savings for a rainy day (or year), continue to work on innovation for your business, and create multiple streams of income. But I will go into all of this more later.

I was having a really hard time dealing with my emotions. My organization, Fearless Women, had just had an incredible 2019 and we started 2020 with a bang! We had a great opportunity to hold a vision board workshop at the top of 2020 at a women's shelter. We brought together a group of incredible women who shared their stories of trauma and triumph. But who knew that soon after that event our lives would change due to COVID-19 and our vision boards would fade?

My passion is to empower, motivate, help educate, and inspire women. But during the pandemic, I felt numb. I wondered, *What do I say to my tribe? How do I uplift my community and followers?* So many were mourning a family member, struggling with the loss of a job, overwhelmed with having to home school their child(ren), and just feeling anxiety due to the uncertainty. And there were those dark questions: What if someone was now left home alone? What if someone was now stuck in a space where they were being abused? What if some people were not safe? What if some people weren't coping well mentally? Those were all of the questions racing through my mind, especially having dealt with domestic violence myself. I did not know how to approach the COVID-19 pandemic or how to pivot my services. I didn't know how to

HELP. I wanted to be proactive for my community. I wanted to work on self-improvement.

Here are some of the ways I coped and pivoted during COVID-19, as well as some tips and strategies you can use.

Declutter your home. Declutter your mind.

You need to organize and manage your life so that you are in control and you create the energy you need to be productive. You have the power to be in control. You have to be organized in all areas or your disorganization will affect everything else you do. What have you been complaining about that you have not had time to do? What can you do to make your time at home comfortable, empowering, peaceful, and happy? (Well, as happy as we can be.)

I decided to make over my home. Early on in March 2020, I ordered furniture, computer chairs, and desks so that my kids and I could have a workspace to adapt to remote work and remote learning. I painted my entire apartment and added other small details that would set the tone for what, at that point, was 10 months (December 2020) from when the COVID-19 outbreak began. After doing those things, I started feeling hope again. I knew it was time for me to share that hope with my tribe, community, and supporters. But doing so was not easy as I was still going through the motions.

I started to experience multiple emotions centered around feeling defeated, like I was not doing enough. Then, I started having conversations with close friends who were having trouble pivoting; they were questioning their own productivity level and comparing themselves to others. The term imposter syndrome started to come up a lot in conversations. We felt insecure. How could we thrive as others were doing? How did they figure it out? Did we measure up to them? Those were the negative thoughts that were consuming so many. But why? Everyone's journey is completely different. I had to make sure that I was reminding others (and myself) that it was ok to take your time, it was ok to go at your own pace, and it was ok to just use 2020 to take a step back, focus, work on your mindset, and plan.

Take a break from social media.

Why place energy and focus on what others are doing when you can utilize that time for your personal and business growth?

Tell your story.

Let's go back to the drawing board. No matter what type of business you have, there is always a story on why you started and built it. Think of these questions when you are going through a transitional time: What is your story? Who are you? What is your purpose? Everyone has one. The answers to these questions are extremely important as they are the blueprint to marrying your passion and your business. Knowing your WHY will allow you to be genuine and transparent with your services and intentions, and it will create engagement and momentum as not only are you a skilled professional providing great service but now people can relate to you on a personal level as well. That connection will convert to sales and will open the doors for more opportunities. Do you know how many of us are not only providing great service, but are now also speaking on public platforms, writing books, and empowering others? So ask yourself, *What is my story?*

Everything starts with your mindset.

Let go of the things you can't control. To reach your goals and achieve your vision for your life, you need to align all of the parts in your life. You cannot say you want to achieve something great but parts of you are not aligned with that goal. Shift your mindset. Health and fitness became extremely important to me during quarantine. I knew exercising would be essential for my mental health and strength. It became a part of my life and I was so happy to share that with everyone and inspire others to get outdoors, safely. I am grateful to have been able to participate in great mental health workshops and also spearhead one for our staff and the youth at our center.

Check in with your family and friends, your neighbors, your co-workers, and your community.

Now is a perfect time to rebuild relationships that are important to you that have been lost due to our extremely "busy" schedules. I also highly recommend that if you feel like you need to talk to someone, please do so. There is accessible help out there and you are not alone.

Create a consistent daily routine.

You are aware that life is not perfect and there may be temporary setbacks, like the COVID-19 pandemic, that can derail your goals. However, no matter how uncomfortable life may become, you must look at every problem as an opportunity to grow. If you want to reach your goals, you have to create a consistent daily routine for yourself. This may look like waking up at 6:00 a.m., making your bed, brushing your teeth, meditating, making sure you get a workout in, eating a quick healthy breakfast, getting dressed, leaving enough time to relax as to not feel rushed as you make it out of your home, and making sure that you are not reaching for your phone first thing in the morning.

Discipline.

You can't just have discipline in one area of your life. It does not work that way and it is not effective. If you slack in one area, it will influence all other areas. Starting your business, reinventing your business, pivoting your business, etc., requires a strong level of discipline. You have to know that you will have to give up some things and people in order to achieve your goal. Discipline should be a positive habit that becomes a part of your daily life. As we all now know, this COVID-19 time may become a lonely one for you, but it is worth the sacrifice. Too many distractions lead to a lack of productivity. What are you willing to give up to get what you want?

Focus.

You need to build a mindset based on an incredibly strong focus. Your vision should be in your mind constantly. Focus on long-term and monthly goals. This focus will drive you; it will become your superpower. Create a schedule for working on your goals, projects, business plans, mindset, etc. Do not allow for distractions.

Manage your time effectively.

Allow 15-20 minutes for preparation before an interview, meeting, conference call, Zoom, presentation, etc. Test your computer or laptop to make sure it has internet service and you are able to present any documents if need be. And make sure your microphone and camera work.

Be prepared and on time.

Remember that time is your most important commodity. Once it is gone you will never get it back.

Get your business in order.

Take a close look at your business. Are there any loose ends? Are there any things you need to get in order? Do you qualify for small business loans? If not, why not? So many of us are operating our businesses without structure. The way your business structure is set up determines how strong and effective your business is. Hire a professional (within your budget but who is good) and get your business in order. Whether you are an entrepreneur who is employed or unemployed, on your own, or a seasoned vet, you must do things differently in order to survive a shift in business. The good thing is that the fundamentals, such as tenacity, commitment, vision, and basic business skills have not changed. However, new strategies are required.

Some tips for a successful business are: have a written plan, have a plan B, be open to receiving advice from others for ideas and accountability, keep track of everything, delegate, and use the internet for research and reinventing your business.

Pivot.

Pivoting is an opportunity for a new beginning. Embrace the fear of the unknown. Every change you experience allows you the opportunity to add the new knowledge of self into your identity, sense of purpose and into your business. All of the obstacles you overcome and the change your experience will help you grow and become more of who YOU are. Change is a part of life and a part of evolving. Embrace the change you are experiencing and tap into your sense of empowerment, contribution, significance, and belonging. Separate yourself from the challenging experience you are facing. Maintain self-care routines and rituals. Focus on your resilience. Ask for help. Celebrate growth. Reflect on your own unique journey. Connect with your community.

Prior to COVID-19, my creative friends and I always talked about a fully remote work world where we could work from the most beautiful, exotic places that sparked our creativity and passion and allowed us to expand our minds and produce work that was coming from our hearts. Being in corporate America did not allow for that. Millennials have opted for a more laid back, carefree approach to work, in which the surrounding space nurtures creativity. Google also inspired this change and WeWork was an innovator for the remote work space world. Fast forward and here we are now in a remote work world! So amazing! Right?!

The Fearless Show.

I interviewed and connected with a lot of incredible folks when I moved my podcast to IG Live during the COVID-19 pandemic. Everyone shared their experiences of healing and coping and expressed how they wanted to support each other and come together as a community.

Books and Podcasts.

During the COVID-19 pandemic, I wanted to learn, learn, learn. How many books had I been putting off that I had been wanting to read? Too many. Well, that was the perfect time to read them. Again, not only for me but so that I could share with my tribe all that I'd learned and how I was utilizing my time. I networked a lot virtually and learned through many workshops that were led by industry pioneers whom I have always admired. It was so amazing to see how easily accessible those folks were virtually. I am grateful that I was also asked to participate as a speaker in workshops for Google, the Powerful Women in Business organization, and Harlem Community News. I started teaching youth at my center and in college spaces and I did my very first TEDx talk!

The Seven Day Entrepreneurship Program.

I provided a platform for education during the COVID-19 pandemic by putting together a team of experts that touched on areas such as business 101, branding, financing, bookkeeping, taxes, public speaking, marketing, networking, and leadership. All of which are areas that are super important when starting your business. That workshop actually turned out to be a bit of a challenge as now the competition shifted to the virtual space and I was competing with other workshops. I learned that the PIVOT would not be as easy as I initially thought. Nonetheless, I was up for the challenge and am learning from what went wrong, what went right, and what needs improvement in our new virtual space.

Virtual networking spaces.

There are so many great networking spaces that improved the way we interacted during the COVID-19 pandemic. I encourage you to check them all out. Here are a few: LinkedIn, Instagram, Facebook, Google, Meetup, Clubhouse, Teams, Meet, Hangouts, Zoom, and WebEx. At the end of 2020, it became clear that people naturally crave human interaction, and it is hard to contain a population during a pandemic when folks do not prefer to be alone. I spoke with single individuals who have no children and no significant other, single individuals who do not live with their families, individuals stuck in domestic violence or abusive situations, elderly people who were not able to see their families, and those of us who dealt with the loss of family members and friends. We all shared a commonality—loneliness.

The year 2020 was devastating. The stories of loneliness and loss reminded me of how we take for granted our time with our family and friends. Now I see some hope, but I also see many who are still struggling with no work, no cash flow, no home, losing their home, no focus, devastation, and so much sorrow. Our country is also dealing with another major issue which is racism, and everyone is in an uproar with the lack of humanity. But the positive side to this is that YOU can do something to help by strengthening your business and empowering your community with the knowledge and resources needed to sustain our neighborhoods, build wealth, inspire our youth, and take our power back. United we are stronger.

How I Bobbed and Weaved Through the Pandemic Like a Beast!

Melissa Cisco

I was born in Manhasset which is located on the north shore of Long Island. I was raised in Roslyn Heights, a small Mayberry-type town not too far from Manhasset. My mother, a young single parent, raised my sister and me in a two-bedroom duplex in an affordable housing complex known as Laurel Homes. To us, it was the projects! My father migrated to New York in the 1960's after his older siblings made the journey during the Great Migration. Before moving to New York, he share-cropped with his parents and siblings in a small farm town in Roper, North Carolina.

My neighborhood was the "village," although I did not fully understand its intrinsic value until I traveled to Senegal, West Africa, in 2001. I was grateful for the community center; it was a safe space for its residents. I attended Roslyn Public Schools. I was an all-county basketball player and I fell in love with boxing after watching this teenager from Brownsville become the youngest heavyweight boxer in the world. He was a big inspiration to me since he too lost his mother at a young age. I thought to myself, *If he can make it, so can I.* I still admire him to this day.

I have amazing memories with my grandfather who was affectionately known as Grandaddy Chubby. He served in World War II as a cook in the segregated Army. He taught me how to clove a ham when I was five years old and how to bake macaroni and cheese in a cast iron skillet. One day he told me that I would be a lawyer. So, that's what I did. No questions asked. Despite all the obstacles, I attended college and law school. In fact, I was the first college and law school graduate in my immediate family.

I learned about the New York real estate landscape having closed over two thousand residential loans. I decided to leave Long Island. In 2003, without ever stepping foot in the building, I purchased a brownstone in Brooklyn. It was something straight out of a horror movie. I did not care. I was confident that it would be a great investment. Over the years, I have traveled to over forty-five countries, but I can say with conviction that there is no place in the world like Brooklyn.

From 1999 to 2008, I was heavily into the real estate game. A year before the recession, a friend suggested that I consider applying to a teaching program. At the time, I had burned myself out and was seeking ways to transition out of practicing law full-time. So, I researched the program, applied, and was accepted. As a prerequisite, I enrolled in a master's program and was hired to teach in middle school. As I transitioned into my new career, the market crashed and as a result, my real estate business suffered. I depleted what little I had in savings and was living off of my credit cards.

Although it was tough, I bounced back from the recession. I earned another master's degree in educational leadership, saved and invested money, paid off my credit card debt, and purchased my second home. In addition to attending law school, transitioning into teaching was one of the best decisions I have ever made. As a special education teacher, I worked with students who were classified with learning disabilities. In addition to classroom instruction, I served as a college and career advisor which was an experience I enjoyed immensely. I organized college tours to HBCUs, Ivy Leagues, Division 1 schools, and military academies. I organized international trips for students to Africa, Europe, and South America as my school's international studies coordinator.

After twelve years in the classroom, I pursued other opportunities in the education field. I applied for and was offered a new position within our central offices. Two weeks before my last day at the high school, we learned of a new disease from Wuhan, China. We watched as the disease spread across Asia to other continents. At the pace at which the disease spread, I strongly believed the disease was airborne although it had not been confirmed. It made its way to New York City with a vengeance. As infection rates increased, teachers sought union support and called for schools to close. My last day at the school was March 13, 2020. On that day, attendance was low as several students showed signs of sickness. I knew I would miss my Model Congress delegation; I had worked hard to build that team over the previous four years. I decided to have a pizza party for my eighth period class. All of the students surprised me with a signed card which warmed my heart. I wished March 13, 2020, was officially the last day of classes for the year. I was overwhelmed with guilt. After the pizza party, I visited the railcar lab and the college and career office. I packed my things, said goodbye to my classroom at around 6:00 p.m., and left the building with my things in a shopping cart.

Over the weekend, I made a beeline to Macy's since there was a dress code for my new position. I had given away most of my "lawyer suits" after I transitioned into teaching. I'd promised never to wear those uncomfortable clothes again, but I found myself in a position of having to wear something other than college and career shirts with jeans. I picked up several suits, several blazers, and a dress. I was both physically and mentally exhausted. On my way home, I prayed to God for more time to prepare for the job. I wished that I had at least two weeks but, in my mind, that would be impossible. My blood pressure had risen, and I had many things to do before my first day. There just was simply not enough time to complete all of the tasks that I had. Again, I prayed for more time.

On Monday, March 16, 2020, I woke up and learned that the mayor had closed all New York City schools. The infection rate in New York City was five percent as we transitioned from brick and mortar to remote learning. I assumed schools would reopen within two weeks. I began my new position on March 17, 2020. What a time to start a new job! The subway ride to Chambers Street was pretty empty and the trains were very dirty. I noticed that most of the passengers had scarves around their mouths. I do recall that there was a shortage of masks and gloves at that time. I began to cough. Of course, everyone on the train looked at me as if they wanted to throw me out of the car. I actually coughed throughout that day which was very strange because I cough like twice a year. I coughed nervously at work. I assumed the coughing was due to allergies, so I drank a lot of water during that day. I continued coughing for three days, but I was not concerned since I had no COVID-19 symptoms. I was too distracted by the magnificent view of the Brooklyn Bridge from my desk.

During that time, I met with the human resources director, completed a request to work remotely, and by Thursday, I received a laptop and was instructed to work remotely until further notice. After I arrived home from my first day of work, my husband informed me that he had symptoms. I contacted my doctor but was told he was not seeing patients with symptoms and suggested we go to urgent care. We went to urgent care but to no avail. I called several urgent care centers, but no one had the test. A breakthrough came from a doctor in Long Island who told me about an urgent care in Suffolk County. We confirmed an appointment—three days away and an hour drive; we had no choice.

The following day, while I ate Frosted Flakes for breakfast, my husband told me that his boss called and informed him that he tested positive and that he and the others on their team could not report to work. He recommended an urgent care in Howard Beach that had made arrangements to test all union workers. Of course, I thought to myself, *Why must we drive all the way to Howard Beach to get tested?* I am sure you figured out why. In any event, I put on my "Long Island Katie" voice and called the urgent care. We immediately scheduled an appointment for one o'clock that afternoon. After our unsuccessful attempts at finding a place to test, we'd finally hit the jackpot! Back to my Frosted Flakes. I tried to finish my cereal, but I noticed it tasted like cardboard. I had no time to finish, so I left the bowl in the sink and we dashed out to Howard Beach. After my husband was tested, we stopped for lunch. The sandwich and fries I ordered tasted like cardboard. I thought to myself, *What is going on with the food today? Everything tastes like cardboard.* Suddenly, I recalled hearing that one of the symptoms was a loss of taste. Before we left the parking lot, I called the same urgent care again in my "Long Island Katie" voice and scheduled an appointment for a test. Within three days, my husband and I both learned that we were COVID-19 positive. Although we heard that eighty percent of the people who tested positive would recover, we were both very scared. My concern was that we would be part of the twenty percent who died.

I nursed my husband, but it became increasingly difficult for me to walk. I felt as though a grapefruit was lodged in my throat and someone had pushed it down further into my chest. I had no appetite, uncontrollable coughing, and severe fatigue. I could not sleep because I was too scared to close my eyes, since I believed that if I closed my eyes I would die. For three straight days, I could not walk, not even to the bathroom. By that time, my husband felt better and nursed me. I refused to go to the hospital; I honestly did not believe I would be treated fairly as a woman of color, so I made the decision to stay home and ride it out. I was too scared to tell people that I was positive because of the fear of being ostracized. It almost felt like the time of the AIDS epidemic, and I thought I would never again feel the way I felt when I lost members of my family to AIDS.

Every day I learned of the deaths of family members and close friends. I was devastated when my pastor tested positive. I prayed and cried for days. It became hard to watch the news because I wondered if I would be next. I could barely walk for a month and a half. I struggled to sit at the table to work. When I finished work at 5:00 p.m., I was in the bed by 5:02 p.m. I just did not have energy. But I was determined to fight my way through.

It took some time, but I was eventually able to walk on my own again. I regained my appetite, weight, and some energy. My recovery has been slow and my memory is not what it used to be, although it has improved. I can walk up to five miles, but I struggle to breathe. These days, I can only run one lap around the track. But with God's grace, I will be able to run a mile again. I prayed my way through the pandemic and believed that God would spare my life. I honestly believed that there was much more work for me to do for the kingdom.

As a result of my COVID-19 experience, I created an eight-year retirement plan which included me purchasing some land so that I can grow my own food, have my own water, and totally live off the land. I also created a digital portfolio of my assets and documents and shared it with my sister. It includes all of my insurance policies, annuities, pensions, credit card information, deeds, student loan information, and social security statements. I filed my outstanding tax returns and paid the balance to the IRS since I did not want to be garnished by the Feds. I changed my contributions for my annuities/401k plans, added another Roth IRA to my portfolio, and I purchased some stock. I scanned most of my files. I am only about eighty percent digital, so there is still more to do. I also developed a strong desire to become a minimalist.

What did I learn from the pandemic? God answers prayers no matter how impossible they may be! You have to be prepared in and out of season. Not only do you have to save for a rainy day, but you also now have to add recessions and pandemics to your list! Due to many past traumatic experiences, I developed resilience by "bobbing and weaving" through crisis after crisis. During the pandemic, it became necessary to make my mental health a priority. Order always reveals the chaos in your life. As I evaluated my life, I became less of a procrastinator; I experience less stress when I plan ahead. No has become my favorite word. I also learned that minimalism is amazing, but it takes time to get there. As I worked on myself, I wanted to find a way to be a blessing after seeing the horror stories from some families who faced evictions during the pandemic. So, I created a small group of women who were interested in purchasing their first home and others that were interested in investing in real estate. Owning a home has always been linked to financial stability and is viewed as the quickest way to build wealth in this country. I am on a mission to help as many people of color as I can with creating a plan to build wealth so that they can always be recession and pandemic ready.

My life has become less stressful but there are still some things I am learning to let go of, like toxic relationships with family members and friends that simply suck the life out of you. Everyone does not deserve a courtside seat in your life. Some people can be loved from the nosebleed seats.

Although international travel was limited in 2020, I am most proud of the gift I received—two and a half acres of land in Kenya to build a library for students. I am proud of the house I built in Uganda and the one I built in Kenya. I also saw my favorite boxer lace up the gloves one more time, for now. I survived COVID-19 and I am ready for my next season.

Pandemic Perseverance:
Lemons or Lemonade?

Michelle Jenkins

I am the last born of my late mother's eight children. I am a 55-year-old mother of two adult children. Six years ago, I moved to Albany, New York, from Brooklyn, New York, to further my education. I enrolled in an education graduate program at the University at Albany on a full scholarship from Medgar Evers College. I teach early childhood education in an urban community elementary school in one of the most poverty-stricken areas in Albany, and I love what I do. Somehow, teaching during regular school hours was only a part of my desire to contribute to change by helping school-aged children. After a long eight hours of working with four- and five-year-old students (some that require additional support), I coordinate the afterschool and summer programs at various schools within the district. I just completed a much-anticipated online graduate program at Grand Canyon University, a Christian university located in Arizona, and I am one internship away from completing a second graduate program at the University at Albany.

I cannot explain how I became somewhat addicted to education. I have faced and overcome many challenges in my life throughout my educational journey. As a result of teaching and learning, I continued to develop the desire and self-determination to persevere in my role as an educator regardless of any challenges or barriers, including COVID-19. As a child growing up in an urban community, I never imagined going to college. As I grew older, I never took the time to think about what the future had in store for me as an African American woman. My mother gave me two choices when I completed high school. She said, "Either you get a job or you go back to school." I'd struggled throughout high school because I was always a social butterfly, so going back to school was completely out of the question. Fortunately, back in the days, it was more of who you knew rather than what you knew. I attended a business school for one year, started having children, and landed myself a few administration jobs. Those jobs led to a variety of management positions from fast food to industrial companies to corporate America. Without any secondary education and with two babies, I was making an upper middle-class salary before

I was 25. Then along came the first real crisis I would face.

My mother was the hero in our family. She raised eight children, mostly as a single parent. She provided everything we needed and most of what we wanted, as long as we earned it, then she retired after working over 30 years at the telephone company and only got to enjoy five years of her retirement. She mostly stayed at home and ate ice cream before she unexpectedly started forgetting things. She suffered with dementia for several years which evolved into full-blown Alzheimer's, causing her to need 24-hour supervision. The hospital visits and hospital stays increased, she could not recognize any of her children, and family decisions had to be made regarding her health and well-being. Out of eight children, it was really just my sister and I who were willing to care for her. It was a hard decision to make, but I quit my job to care for my mother while my sister continued to work. My mother's illness was our family's first crisis and I felt that I had to make that change in my life to care for her.

While doing so, I became extremely depressed. I was already going through my own personal crisis—overcoming a sixteen-year relationship and breakup with a man half my age. Although I was sad, broken, depressed, and now jobless, I never gave up. As a Christian woman, my faith in God has always been my strength. But God does His part in the spiritual realm, and we must do our part in the natural realm. I had to find a way to turn that crisis into an opportunity for me to keep going, growing, and glowing. But the more thought I put into it, the more I would reach a dead end. I started thinking that maybe I went the wrong direction when I was at the fork in the road of choosing a path. Maybe I was supposed to take my hair styling profession, a side hustle that I enjoyed, to the next level. I was so confused and undecided. It was the prime of my life, I was in my late 30's/early 40's, but I didn't have a solid future or goal. I had the urgent feeling of wanting change for the better—for myself and for my now two young adult children.

While caring for my mother, making ends meet by being a hairstylist was my only means of income. One summer evening, I was doing one of my closest friend's daughter's hair. We were having our usual heartfelt conversations. My friend's daughter was someone I admired from afar; I was not open about how much I admired her accomplishments while she attended Medgar Evers College. It seemed like every other day my friend was calling me to share her daughter's achievements and invite me to the awards ceremonies. I attended them all; they were endless. I must admit, I couldn't explain the feeling of admiration, and even a little jealousy, that I felt because it was not my children or me who had made such strides in education.

As I was adding the finishing touches to her hair, I was sharing with her how lost I felt, how I felt like I had failed my children, and how my mother being sick and having to take care of her was affecting my life in such a negative way. She asked me with compassion, care, and concern, "Auntie Chell, why don't you take this time to go back to school?" That one question turned my entire life around. It was the beginning of my urgent desire to persevere. She went on to tell me how much she admired me for working in managerial positions, being a single mother, and taking care of my mother. She told me that I had everything in me that it would take to be a successful college student. She is now my mentor, a sociology professor, and a bestselling author.

Education was never really a focus of mine, regardless of how much my mother promoted its importance. Astonishingly, I returned to school to further my education after a 28-year absence. That was my first experience of overcoming a crisis, and the beginning of a long journey of overcoming unexpected crises. None of which were as unexpected as the COVID-19 pandemic.

Like others, I believed that the pandemic would have negative outcomes for people, especially

African Americans, until I realized that education would be the tool I used to make lemonade with the lemons that were thrown at me during that time.

When life throws you lemons, find a way to use those lemons to make lemonade. Think about the negative energy in your circle and the environments you frequent. Write down the names of those negative people and places. Then think about the positive people and places in your life and write them down. As if you were figuring out a puzzle, write down everything you can possibly think of that can move the negatives to the positive side. One thing that I have learned as a student and a professional is that writing things down makes all the difference; there is something serene about seeing your thoughts on paper. Apply this strategy to create a recipe for using the lemons in your life to make lemonade.

I was thrown lemons when I started my first graduate program. I met all of the requirements, completed all of the courses, and passed all of the exams, except math. Math has always been a barrier for me to become a certified educator. I knew I had to start over and take a different path, but I was unsure of what that path would be. I made lemonade with those lemons when I decided to enroll in a different graduate program that did not include math courses. I was thrown lemons when I was the only older African American student in all of my classes which made me feel like quitting because I did not fit in. I made lemonade with those lemons when I sat at the front of the class and took every opportunity to raise my hand to have a say whenever the topic of African Americans not being able to succeed because of their socioeconomic status came up.

I was thrown lemons when I realized I had to teach under the same curriculum as other teachers for half the pay because I was not certified. I made lemonade with those lemons by teaching students that were the children of professors and other professionals that worked right on the very campus where I took classes. I was thrown lemons when I celebrated my brother's homecoming from serving a 22-year sentence in prison for defending his own and he eventually passed from a heart attack in his sleep after being home for eight short years. I made lemonade with those lemons by embracing the time we had together. I had encouraged him to start over. Subsequently, he began a career as a head chef at a well-known soul food restaurant in Manhattan. Within months of losing one brother, COVID-19 unexpectedly took the life of my eldest brother.

How was I going to make lemonade out of those lemons? How could I maintain my desire for perseverance? One may not believe that persevering in the midst of a crisis is possible. But right in the midst of mourning my brothers, I knew it was time for change and self-reflection.

I consider myself to be the curious type. I always have questions about everything; there is no topic for which I don't want to know who, what, when, where, and why. Hearing about COVID-19 on the news ignited my curiosity which caused me to transition into a bed bum. I would get home from work, take a shower, grab a bite to eat, then watch every news channel and surf the web on my phone. I wanted to know everything there was to know about the virus, which was getting more and more serious as the days went by. The first real wind that blew me over during the pandemic was literally being thrown out of my classroom on a Friday. I never imagined that I would not be returning for months. Working from home and pivoting into virtual teaching did not help. Eventually, I stopped grabbing bites to eat and I stopped answering phone calls. It was like I was in the COVID-19 twilight zone.

Although we were advised to stay home, I became obsessed with the supermarket, afraid that the world was coming to an end and not wanting to die from hunger. My savings started dwindling down and then the financial strain surfaced.

Psychologically, I was changing but not for the better. I was concerned about my mental and physical health, paranoid that if I had so much as a sniffle or scratchy throat that I had been infected. I was right at the beginning of the second semester of my program. Until the pandemic, education was my medicine for everything. I always wanted more information and knowledge, specifically about the history of my own culture. Unfortunately, I was not interested in my studies and fell way behind. I could not focus enough to write any papers or complete any assignments.

The light bulb finally went off after being depressed and homebound for a few months. I went to my notebook and found what I wrote down about my negatives and positives. I realized that on that list my positives outweighed my negatives. I was confused because with the presence of COVID-19 nothing felt positive, so I started writing new lists. To my surprise, even in the midst of a pandemic, I was still thriving and pivoting. The more I analyzed my lists of all the things I thought about and the things I wrote down, I began to focus on what could contribute to changing the negatives into positives. I realized that everything positive I thought about was grounded in my self-determination and resilience to persevere in being an educator.

My studies were grounded in the changes within societies—globally and locally. Sociology was the perfect course to take at that time. I learned so much about the history of oppression that my ancestors faced, and the sociological perspectives that were created to try to explain the past, present, and future of society's downfalls. I learned how our nations have a history of politically incorrect politicians and that globally racism and inequality are still very present. I was able to observe the unfortunate series of events—the rioting and protesting that took place—with a renewed mind and knowledge about my own culture. Those events encouraged me to read every peer reviewed and scholarly article put before me. I conducted my own research and learned that I was completely miseducated. So, I decided that as an education change agent, I would take what I learned and ease it into whatever curriculum I was instructed to design. My theory is that by educating prospective teachers, even if I only get through to a few of them without miseducating them, those few teachers will teach a classroom full of students, and those students will grow up with the truth and be positive additions to society.

I came up with my theory over 10 years ago, the moment I decided to further my education and was accepted into the SEEK (Search for Education,

Elevation, and Knowledge) program at Medgar Evers College. The SEEK program provides additional academic and financial support to first time freshmen. It was key to me being in an environment that allowed me to learn the truth about the history of my culture. Coming up with a theory on how I could contribute to change and become a change agent within our education system was the turning point I had been praying for. The power of prayer is amazing, and it is truly my faith in God that carries me. From that point on, I turned the television off, focused on my studies, and revisited my list frequently to ensure that I was still thriving.

The questions I will continue to ask myself in the midst of any crisis are: *How can I use the lemons that life throws at me to make sweet, successful lemonade? How can I make a difference? In what ways can I continue to make a change?* Not everyone is a student, so education may or may not be the tool that you can use to make lemonade out of lemons. It really does not matter who you are, or what you do, you have the ability to persevere during a pandemic. Find your tool, write it down, make your lists, revisit the lists, and edit the lists when necessary. And keep in mind that making lemonade out of lemons takes some footwork, self-determination, and unlimited prayer.

Shining Through the 2020 Pandemic

Lakeasha Williams

I exploded onto the education scene in 2018 and hit the ground running as a new principal. I was appointed to the position on June 26, 2018. I went to work on June 27, 2018. The Shine Shine 399 school community accomplished many great things our first year together. We cultivated a new team overall; developed our school mantra ("Empowered, Engaged, Enlightened, Exceptional"); and embarked on defining our comprehensive academic, social, and emotional learning program. Shine Shine 399 was born! In year one, I was rated a well-developed rookie principal after just 60 short days of being a new leader in a school that was ranked number 29 out of 32 schools in the district. That same year, we also created teacher impact teams throughout the school community, empowered our families in a variety of ways, and used data to drive our instruction to meet the needs of our scholars. Also, in year one, I was handsomely awarded the esteemed recognition of Patricia

Mcguirk Principal of the Year! That recognition was an AMAZING culminating accomplishment for a first year principal!

Then entered March madness 2020. So many unexpected events took place during that time that shook my foundation to the core. First, I had to get an emergency medical procedure that caused me to miss the first week of school during that month. I went back to work at 65 percent capacity while also thinking that it was time to reevaluate my work-play balance for a higher quality of life. Never did I imagine I would be catapulted into that realm with the rising of COVID-19 cases, the heightened alert for New York City, and the subsequent city shut down including school closures. I feared that all we accomplished in such a short time span would be compromised with the closure of schools. We had three days to prepare for remote learning. Many things raced through my mind. My staff was predominantly technologically challenged. How would we manage? My children were beginning to show academic, social, and emotional progress. How would remote learning impact their continued progress? My families were finally feeling supported. How could we continue to provide an adequate level of support in the remote world? Although my body was still in physical pain, I returned to work and went straight into beast mode. I had to show up for my school community.

My school was in a frenzy during those three days! One of our school partners provided technology workshops to our staff each day. It was important that our staff felt comfortable navigating Google Classroom and providing support to our children and families in the virtual world. We distributed 70 percent of our newly acquired technology devices to our scholars. We had to ensure the continuity of instruction for our children. Teachers were gathering up the necessary resources they would have to take home to continue instruction. I was downloading, uploading, saving, and sending to myself a variety of data and materials that would allow me to continue successfully in my role as principal from home. We also practiced safety measures during that time to ensure the well-being of all of our staff members. We did not know what to expect from the COVID-19 virus and how it would impact our lives and health overall. However, I remained steadfast in my leadership role and focused on one goal—functioning as a cohesive school in the remote world. We would no longer be together in the physical school building, but we would remain together in spirit in the remote world.

It broke my heart that children were in school one day and schools were closed the next day. When they left the building on Friday, March 13, 2020, we had no idea that school would be closed on Monday. As I walked my building, I saw notebooks, personal items, and classrooms ready to receive children. I wondered, *How are my children doing? How will they cope with this sudden disruption to what was considered normal?* Remote learning of this magnitude was also new to our school system, but I knew that we had to make sure that we engaged with our children daily. The teachers and I collaborated on a school schedule that was fair for our children. We knew that parents were not teachers by trade and it was important for us to continue in our roles as the educators, but I was extremely worried. My school had some challenging years over the past decade. We were beginning to make some traction. We were shining once again. What would this school closure really mean for our children? Our school demographics reflect 27 percent of students in temporary housing, 12 percent special education, 12 percent English as a new language, and a high poverty rate overall. We needed additional support services prior to the global COVID-19 pandemic. I was afraid of what remote learning would mean for our school community moving forward.

We left the building at the end of those three days and it was time to make my home a dual workplace, but I was still not 100 percent well physically. My body came crashing down for some much-needed rest and recovery. How was I going to juggle taking care of my health, motivate my staff to keep going, as well as serve our scholars and families well from home? Everyone had questions but I did not have answers. All I knew was that we had to show up for our children. Our shining stars were depending on us to be there for them no matter what. That thought became my go-to motivation during a time when I was just as afraid as everyone else.

Next, it was time to log on to Google Classroom to begin our virtual school experience. But how was I going to lead a school with an emotionally charged staff? The global COVID-19 pandemic had everyone on pins and needles, and rightfully so! How could I center myself so that I could be what my school community needed me to be? I thought about the doctors, nurses, and everyone in the healthcare field who faced death and sicknesses daily. I thought about the essential workers who could not work from home and had to take jam-packed public transportation to and from work each day. I thought about the millions of people having to apply for unemployment. That line of thinking really put things into perspective for me. There was no way that I could wallow in what I felt was self-pity with so much despair all around me. I proceeded to work delicately with my staff to impart that same notion. We were experiencing sickness and death all around us. We were home and quarantined from extended family and friends. Life as we knew it had ceased to exist. Yet, we still had to show up for our children and families.

I most definitely understood my staff's trepidations. I was ready to incorporate modifications to make things more feasible for everyone. I revised our school schedule to also account for wellness for staff, added additional preparation time due to the technology expectations, and continued professional development support for our staff. The administrative team also continued to build our teaching and learning structures to ensure the continued success of our children in the remote world. Initially, we had our struggles. But after continued collaboration, we were united in our efforts to make remote learning a success for our school community. And succeed we did!

We missed our families tremendously! They were very hands-on with our school turnaround efforts from the very beginning. They volunteered regularly at the school. They conducted fundraisers, wrote grants, attended community walks, and did whatever was necessary to support all of our children. How were we going to modify our family engagement efforts to ensure continued active participation? The COVID-19 pandemic meant that we had to redefine support. Sometimes that meant just listening to parents vent their frustrations regarding what life would look like after COVID-19. During the height of the pandemic, everyone was overwhelmed. We wanted to be a source of comfort and support for our families so we provided wellness checks; a variety of academic, social, and emotional support; and a weekly food contribution as well. Our families expressed their gratitude for maintaining a sense of normalcy in their lives during what was a very traumatic time.

The sense of community is prevalent in our school. Once we established a sense of normalcy, we were able to extend our gratitude to others. Our school community wanted to live up to our school mantra ("Empowered, Engaged, Enlightened, Exceptional"), so we decided to conduct a car parade to express our thanks and appreciation for all of the essential workers in our community. The participants included scholars, staff, families, and community leaders. We hit the streets together and proceeded to the local supermarket, post office, recreational center, hospitals, and our local precinct. Our "Thank you, Essential Workers" car parade was well received by our community neighbors! Most importantly, it had a profound effect on those of us who participated. Volunteering has many benefits including allowing you to connect to your community to make it a better place, bolstering confidence, networking, and achieving an overall sense of accomplishment. We were once again united in our efforts. Everything that we do is for our children, our shining stars! They are the center of every decision that is made as well.

We continued to provide academic support to our scholars. But we also knew the importance of ensuring that our children were emotionally well. They too were experiencing trauma because of the global COVID-19 pandemic. We afforded our children the opportunity to participate in individual and group therapy sessions as needed. Under the leadership of our guidance counselor and social worker, our children engaged in weekly social and emotional learning activities. Our classroom teachers also provided daily wellness checks as they transitioned between the academic subjects. I also knew the importance of securing additional partnerships so that our shining stars could receive enrichment support such as attending virtual Broadway shows and trips as well as robotics and dance. We also had a weekly reading explosion where we invited special guests to read to our scholars. Everyone would wait eagerly to meet the guest reader and hear them read aloud. It was reminiscent of going to the movie theater for our school community. Immersing ourselves in school-wide activities helped us to remain united as a school family.

How was I able to effectively lead my school community and shine during a global pandemic? I had to first get my emotional and physical well-being together. I was now home every day after working an average of 12-hour days for almost two years and attending a variety of community meetings and events. My work schedule was hectic! I was never home. My goal as a new principal was to network as much as possible so that my school could receive much-needed resources, programs, and services. But working at that pace was beginning to take a toll on my health. New York City's shutdown meant that I was at home more than I ever was in my adult life! It was the perfect opportunity for me to focus on my mental state and overall health.

How was I able to push through? I started walking several times during the week. The fresh air and sun did wonders for my soul! I started working out virtually with a trainer. I was cooking my own food and eating healthier meals. I was able to meditate, stretch, and drink my green tea each morning. You cannot pour from an empty cup. For me to effectively lead my school community, I had to first take care of me.

How was I able to hold on? I have a resilient tunnel vision for achieving my goals. It is important to focus on your overall goal, create an action plan, and hold yourself accountable with progress checks along the way. Also, celebrate your interim levels of success throughout the process. Give yourself opportunities to allow for downtime as well. That helps to maintain a level of balance in your life.

The global COVID-19 pandemic helped me to see the value of self-care. If we want to be successful in our professional lives, we must also be successful in our personal lives. Although COVID-19 was an unimaginable tragedy, I was still able to learn some valuable life lessons. I learned to put me first. Taking care of yourself is not a selfish act, it is mandatory. Do not sweat the small stuff. It may sound cliché, but the COVID-19 pandemic taught us that health, family, and love are far more important than anything else. Working together with everyone across our school community also reaffirmed my belief in humanity.

Although my school community is still engaged in turnaround efforts, we were able to persevere and ensure that we served our scholars, families, and community at large. Our entire school community also demonstrated empathy skills and gave back to each other and our larger community. The COVID-19 experience led us to our school's year three theme: "United We Stand (Scholars, Families, Staff, Community)."

Striving in Uncertainty

Shatema Reedy

Throughout life, we tend to seek a stamp of approval, a sign, or direction for what we should do next. For example, my daughter was being evaluated because I noticed some delays and it turned out that she was diagnosed at two-and-a-half with mild autism spectrum disorder. The evaluation lasted for about three hours, then I waited to hear the results from the resident and chief neurologist. Once I found out that she did have autism, the neurologist told us (myself and her dad) to set up an appointment with her pediatrician to seek early intervention practices. Once we received the necessary information, we made an appointment and had an evaluation done by one of the speech therapists at her daycare. One of the questions she asked me was, "Does your child seek to be praised?" At first I thought to myself, *Well, shouldn't I raise my child to be humble instead of prideful?* What the therapist meant was that children seek approval.

They want to know that someone is in their corner. It makes them feel loved and important in their own little world.

Most, if not all, of us were faced with many obstacles and challenges, especially in 2020. Every day, we saw the news media capturing frightening moments regarding something that we had never experienced before. Something that we really didn't have knowledge or foreknowledge about. How did COVID-19 come into existence? Where did it originate? There were many questions but no definitive answers. What we know is that we saw the effects of the virus—many were sick, cases rose, and over 223,000 people left this earth.

Similarly, there is no definitive answer for autism. For those who have loved ones that have been diagnosed, information changes every day. Even though we have advanced developmentally using medical and psychological practices for ASD, the thought of my child continuing to live with this diagnosis and being unsure of how she will live independently once she gets older brings added stress. Living with uncertainty can be a bit challenging and overwhelming. It can change the whole atmosphere in your life causing you to wonder, "What is my reason for living?"

I want to bring your attention to some things that may encourage you while you are trying to strive in a season of uncertainty.

1. No one knows everything!

For some of us, planning our lives out to the extreme brings about a sense of control and stability, and removes all anxiety. It creates a safe space for us to set and accomplish our goals. My daughter is a person of strict scheduling and routines. Individuals who are on the spectrum tend to have a hard time transitioning from one task to the next. For them to do so will sometimes require therapeutic directives, meticulous scheduling, and planning. For example, I remember picking my daughter up from daycare one day. I would usually take the same way home; however, on that particular day, I needed to go grocery shopping. So, I proceeded to drive off from the daycare and I made a different turn.

My daughter started to scream! I immediately pulled the car over panicking, not even sure what to think at that moment. We had to sit there for about five minutes and I had to figure out what was wrong. Even though she was verbal, she could not really verbalize what was wrong and she could not explain to me what made her feel uncomfortable. I finally realized what was wrong—I was not taking the same way home. I did not tell her that we were going grocery shopping first. Of course I was saying to myself, *Who's the parent and who's the child?!* I didn't even know that I had to explain myself about where I, the adult, was going! Yes, you're supposed to laugh there.

As I look back at that moment with her and think about where the world is now, I see that many of us are facing the unexpected. Due to the COVID-19 pandemic, most of us had to adjust to uncomfortable situations such as: becoming "teacher-parents," learning technology (for those who are not technologically savvy), and creating more of a planned-out schedule to have some type of normalcy. But you are doing it. See what I said there?! YOU'RE DOING IT! Give yourself a pat on the back!

One thing I can say is that when we are at our lowest point or feel like we cannot go on, there is an adrenaline rush that comes over us so that we can push forward, especially in times of the unknown. For me, this journey is a faith walk. For some, life just may be that you are not becoming stagnant in this journey because you know what it feels like to get stuck and you are determined to move. Even in your determination, you still may not have the information you need but keep pushing forward and you will get it. Sometimes, we are put to the test to see how much determination we have within ourselves. There is an inner strength that exudes out of you.

2. Breathe!

According to Merriam Webster Dictionary, the word breathing comes from breathe which is "to draw air into and expel it from the lungs; to take in oxygen and give out carbon dioxide through natural processes." Why am I bringing up the word breathe or breathing? Some of us have not taken a breath of fresh air since the COVID-19 pandemic began. As a matter of fact, some of us have had loved ones pass away because their breath was taken away from them by the virus. My aunt, for example, succumbed to complications from the virus and passed away six days after my birthday. It was such a devastating loss. However, I was comforted by my belief that Heaven is her eternal home. While my aunt was here on Earth, she taught me life lessons, especially when my daughter was diagnosed with ASD. Sometimes I would call her because I wasn't understanding how to tackle the diagnosis. I wasn't in denial, but I was trying to understand what I needed to do as a parent to ultimately make my daughter self-sufficient. In a calm voice, she always used to say, "BREEEAAATTTHHHHEEEEE!"

As I mentioned earlier in the definition of breathing, the latter part states that you "take in oxygen and give out carbon dioxide." We have all had situations, especially in 2020, that figuratively knocked the wind out of us and left us feeling like we couldn't breathe. From the Coronavirus to systemic racism to politics to protests, and many personal things, breathing has not been easy because we have not been able to comfortably exhale. Some of us are still holding our breath. Some of us have the mentality of that famous saying, "It ain't over until the fat lady sings." Many of us are still waiting to hear her sing aloud! While you're waiting for that, breathe!

As you can see, the world has not stopped, so you cannot stop! I've had to ask myself often, *What would happen to my daughter if I did not proactively seek help with her diagnosis?* So many of us have been stagnant in our daily lives because we're simply not breathing through the changes of life. We must keep breathing even when we don't understand what is going on. Don't you notice that when you don't get to properly exhale, you tend to have more heightened anxiety and fear? Listen, as many jobs as each of us have, whether it is a nine to five, home schooling, or being an entrepreneur, we cannot afford not to breathe.

Our actions will often determine our future. Everyone has their own methods of getting through rough seasons in their lives. For me, remote learning was a hard decision to make. As I mentioned, my child has mild ASD and she was accepted into a new program at a new school. During the summer of 2020, I was contemplating blended learning. However, science had not lied about the COVID-19 pandemic. So, I opted for my daughter to be fully remote at home. Of course, like many parents, I wondered if I was making the best decision for her. I wondered to myself if she was going to get the education and services she needed. In March 2020, when the virus started in New York City, everyone was sent home and children began learning remotely. Everything wasn't thought-out at first, but educators knew that they had to do something immediately. There were over a million school kids at home! Children didn't know what to do. Parents didn't know what to do. It was pure chaos that was abruptly handed to all of us. However, when we were all faced with challenges, some of us cried, screamed, and felt like it was unfair, especially to the children.

Now, remember how I told you that my child doesn't adapt to transitioning well? So, here we were again. I had another situation, but I'd learned from the other experience that I had to explain to her what was going on so that she could at least get an idea of what was happening and what was to come. At first, it seemed as though she understood. Wow, I was so happy to see that there weren't any outbursts, uncontrollable tantrums, or anything! I thought to myself that I'd finally mastered that hurdle. Needless to say, when the first day of remote learning happened, I failed miserably.

I woke my daughter up at her regular time for school, got her ready, put on her uniform shirt to create some type of normalcy for her, and as soon as remote learning started she said to me in a stern voice, "I am not doing this." I had to look at her because at first I thought, *Wow, you are using your words correctly and speaking so clearly.* But on the other hand, I was saying to myself, *Did she just tell me what she was going to do?* Here we were going again with this thing called control. So, I spoke with her like I'd talked with her that whole weekend and explained to her how the teachers were waiting to see her on the computer. Of course, she was not having any parts of it! So, guess who won that day? She won by a landslide! It was a really rough day; both of us ended up taking naps. But as time went on, my daughter got more comfortable in our new normal.

One thing I noticed about the trying time our world went through in 2020 was that most, if not all, of us were prepared for the unknown. We were not prepared for the devastation, but we were prepared to bounce back even when things still seemed uncertain. Have you ever been through a situation in your life where you thought you were not going to make it and you were reminded that you had gone through something similar and overcame that situation? Some of the tactics you used for those prior experiences may be the keys to you overcoming the obstacles you are facing right now, and the most important one of them all is breathing! Breathe to release the anxiety and tension you feel so that you can conquer the obstacles to come.

3. New beginnings!

As I am writing this, I am reminded that in order to have new beginnings, some old things have to be tossed away. Most of us can honestly say that when we start something new, sometimes we have lingering things that try to attach themselves to us and hinder us from going into our new beginning. Sometimes, the hindrances are things that we caused that we're afraid to let go of. We can learn from them and be reminded of where we came from and the journey that is ahead of us. However, what happens when you can't even sense that there is a new beginning ahead of you?

Remember I mentioned that I lost my aunt in 2020. I recently had another devastating loss—my uncle, my aunt's husband! Eight months apart and now they were both gone. Since I have never been married, I can only imagine what my uncle felt or went through when he lost his soulmate. I do believe that the hurt that he felt compared to none. I look at their situation and it brings many things to mind. They both had health challenges and wanted to be well, but I believe they knew they weren't going to be well here in the physical. Once they both transitioned, it reminded me of what the apostle Paul talks about in 1 Corinthians 15:53b where he said, "the mortal must put on immortality." In order for them to be incorruptible, their corrupted bodies had to die.

In 2020, we dealt with the corruption of COVID-19, police brutality, politics, and so many systemic issues in our country that sometimes we couldn't see the way to a new beginning. However, that path starts with self; we must all do a self-examination. Two of the questions we should ask ourselves are: "What did I learn about myself during the pandemic?" and "What were some of the methods I used to overcome the stress and anxiety I was feeling?" The reason why self-examination is important is because we are compassionate creatures. Our compassion leads to a sense of justice because we know that someone is being helped. However, how can we help others if we do not help ourselves first? In order for me to be a light of encouragement or positivity, I must first learn the art of encouraging myself and building myself up so that I can share that same light with others.

The steps I have shared will help us all become better individuals and cause us to continue striving when uncertainty is ahead!

Man Makes Plans and God Laughs

Deidra Towns

The year 2020 started off with so much promise. I was filled with hopeful expectation for what was sure to be an epic year. How could it be anything else? I had done the work. I had a strategy. I was well resourced. My network was connected. And most importantly, I had the will to make things happen. I had spent the beginning of 2020 busying myself by getting booked to teach the Stress Reset—a methodology for shifting from the Stress Response to the Relaxation Response so you can handle whatever life throws your way with grace and ease. After much planning and preparation, I was looking forward to taking the stage and speaking from the sweet spot where passion meets purpose. But alas, much to my surprise, 2020 had other plans for me (and everyone else). It's a good thing I was prepared.

At the tender age of 19, I spent the summer at my aunt's house in Maryland. In the powder room there was a poem framed and hanging on the wall,

"Desiderata," by Max Ehrmann. It was like reading instructions for life. This line struck me and stayed with me for the rest of my life: "Nurture strength of spirit to shield you in sudden misfortune." Something about that poem and that particular line resonated in me profoundly. It felt like I had found a secret key to unlock a super power. I took the words to heart and set myself on a course to discover as much as I could about nurturing my spirit. It is what kept me sane and on course through the pandemic. Here are a few tips based on what I learned.

Tip one: Put your inspiration where you'll see it every day.

That poem is seared into my memory because I read it every time I went to the bathroom. You want to embody an idea or principle? Look at it every day. It's the same reason you'll never see just one McDonald's commercial. Repetition creates conviction. So, when 2020 went off the rails, even though I was caught off guard by the completely unexpected turn of events, I didn't panic. As you know, when waters get rough, if you panic, you'll surely drown. My consistent spiritual practice had developed the resilience and stability within me to weather life's twists and turns. I didn't know how it was going to go, but I knew losing my head wasn't going to help. Did that knowledge make it easy? Hardly. The still, small voice in my heart reminded me of the immortal words of Public Enemy: "Man plans, God laughs." The world was receiving a collective humbling. By the time April 2020 rolled around, all I could do was watch as those engagements I had set up disappeared into thin air. It was like standing on the shore and seeing money wash away with the tide. Whoo that was hard to watch.

Tip two: Lean into uncomfortability.

Lots of **hard things** made you uncomfortable before you mastered them. Multiplication was hard when you were in the third grade. Mastery comes from leaning into difficult, uncomfortable situations. And when life goes there, it's helpful to remember that you've already done lots of hard things. It will feed your confidence to face the challenge at hand.

After work dried up, I didn't even want to check my emails. I knew what messages were waiting for me and I didn't want to read them. What I was left with was lots of time and space. Weren't we all? Here in New York City, most people were staying in. We were facing the specter of the unknown—a virus no one knew much about. There were many questions like: Where did it come from? How do we protect ourselves? Fear and panic were palpable in the air and emotions are contagious.

Something as benign as a trip to the grocery store became a nerve- wracking adventure. New Yorker's are accustomed to being in close physical proximity to one another, but with the pandemic, you had to be hyper vigilant about not having contact with anyone.

And can we talk about the empty shelves? The only time the grocery store is not adequately provisioned is when we're having a snowstorm. But the COVID-19 pandemic had shelves looking mighty bare. When it started, I had lots of paper goods. So, I didn't run out and buy more. I thought, *It's better to let people without get what they need.* Never in my entire life had I seen grocery store shelves empty for weeks on end. I don't think I saw a bottle of Clorox Clean-Up until November 2020. Social distancing forced me to the back of the Costco to get in line. It took me longer to check out than it took me to put my items in the shopping cart. Every time I was in the store, I was eager to get home to safety, away from all of those people. Each of those seemingly small incursions chipped away at my sense of normalcy. They also eroded my sense of security—that what I needed would be available when I needed it. Those challenges were the most difficult parts of the whole ordeal. They were more significant than the canceled engagements because

I knew that I could pivot my work to online. But if the grocery store ran out of food, what would I do?

While training to become a master teacher of the Stress Reset Methodology, I learned the science behind the Stress Response and the Relaxation Response. The Stress Response is a mental, emotional, and physiological response to a perceived threat. The thing is, the part of the brain that makes this assessment, the amygdala, is the oldest part of the brain. It was the first part of the brain to develop in human evolution and it doesn't have the ability to distinguish between different types of stressors. So, the same response is activated when you're on a hike and see a mountain lion as when you make a big mistake at work and your boss goes off the deep end. In one situation your life is in danger, but not in the other.

The Stress Response a.k.a. Fight-Flight-Freeze-Fawn makes it hard to think clearly, see all of your options, and make good decisions. When activated, you can only see what's wrong which leaves you with irrational, unconscious, reactive choices. Decisions made from this level of thinking generally don't end well. That was exactly the response I felt getting stronger in me as the pandemic continued to ravage the city leaving empty grocery store shelves in its wake. Usually, it's easy to initiate a shift from the Stress Response to the Relaxation

Response because I can see that the response isn't proportional to the stressor. My life isn't in any danger so I can quickly calm my nervous system. But for the first time since I'd begun practicing this work, it felt like I might be experiencing a real existential threat. In stressful situations our thinking is hijacked by the amygdala, so our actions tend to drop into a default response. That is when "nurture strength of spirit to shield you in sudden misfortune" comes in handy. It increases our awareness so that we're more sensitive to when we shift out of the Relaxation Response. The earlier we can catch ourselves reacting from the Stress Response, the faster we can get ourselves back on track. Once I realized where I was headed, I knew exactly what I had to do with all that time and spaciousness that became available because the city was shut down.

First, remember to breathe. It sounds super simple, but sometimes simple things have the most profound effect. It is the simplest, most accessible tool I learned from The Stress Reset Methodology. One of the signals that you're in the Stress Response is shallow breathing. Deep abdominal breathing activates the parasympathetic nervous system. Its main function is to help your body rest and digest the stress. I implemented that by resuming my meditation practice. But meditation wasn't the only time I practiced focused breathing. If I started feeling anxiety waiting in line at the big box store, I gave myself grace and did the deep breathing right there next to the vegetables. The beauty of breath work is that it's discreet. No one has to know you're fighting a battle within yourself.

Second, get active. Physical activity is a great way to move stress through and out of your body. You absolutely don't want to store that energy in your cells. But I wasn't going outside unless it was absolutely necessary. I have older parents with pre-existing conditions. I'm seriously committed to minimizing their exposure. So, I went online and bought a set of jump ropes. Every morning I got up and did a jump rope challenge right in my kitchen.

Third, manage your mindset. With so much time on our hands, our minds can get super creative making up stories. Add in a dose of fear and our imaginations can run wild in the wrong direction. Developing the ability to focus the mind is a valuable practice no matter the circumstances. For me, this works best when I write. So, I got some journals and started writing down all of the things for which I was grateful. It gave my mind a direction on which to focus.

Tip three: Attention amplifies.

When you focus on gratitude, life will give you more reasons to be grateful. The inverse works as well. If you focus on your fears, life will give you more reasons to be fearful. Where you focus your attention is a choice. Choose wisely.

There are many ways to bring yourself into the Relaxation Response. These were the three foundational practices that helped me maintain my sanity and focus throughout the lockdown. Some of the other activities that kept me from spiraling into an abyss if despair were: long luxurious baths, discovering good new music online, reconnecting with old friends on the internet, and laughter (deep belly shaking giggles).

My biggest takeaways from 2020 were make plans, be flexible, and look for the opportunity in whatever comes your way. Once I shifted to the Relaxation Response, 2020 gave me time and space to do some much-needed deep release, forgiveness, and healing. It amplified the value of mind-body-spirit work and reminded me that God's plan is greater than my own. All in all, I am grateful.

You can find the complete Desiderata poem at www.desiderata. com/desiderata.html

Pivoting Through the
Pandemic with Faith

Mecca Nelson

My health and wellness journey started a decade ago while living a military lifestyle. My late husband, Sergeant Nelson, served in the United States Army. I lost my husband while he was serving the country during a mission in Iraq. To deal with his tragic loss, my daughter and I began forging new pathways of strength to conquer our life.

There was a point in my life where I was not able to work for three years due to being injured. During my healing process, I was able to build my business by creating the name, choosing the services I would provide, and deciding the companies and organizations I planned on working with when I launched. Once I was able to return to the workforce, I decided to leap right into my business. I have received numerous accolades and awards, including recognition from elected officials. Having the resilience to pivot through COVID-19 has been an experience for me and my business has flourished in many aspects.

The hardships I faced during COVID-19 were being unable to network with others, postponed and lost contracts, and canceled or rescheduled business trips. I remember the day the governor stated that we would be going into quarantine. I was sitting next to my laptop, preparing an online platform for my classes. After creating the online platform, I took a pause. I needed to take a moment to breathe, reflect, and step away from that particular project. I was receiving multiple phone calls from other business owners requesting my assistance with building a business and I had to cancel a business event that was already planned.

Honestly, I gifted myself a self-care moment for about two weeks before I began to put the pedal to the metal. During that time, I began to virtually teach workshops and network with other individuals. I also continued to build my business. One of the hardships that had me thinking was not generating revenue for 2020. I for one was feeling uncomfortable teaching workshops, networking, and conducting classes through various online platforms such as Zoom, GoToMeeting, Google Hangouts, Blue Jeans Meetings, Cisco Webex Meetings, and others.

I realized I needed to take action by navigating in another direction. I noticed how many individuals were having anxiety attacks and feeling depressed. I also noticed that individuals were reacting to situations emotionally and that domestic violence was escalating. Many individuals were also ending relationships. I was able to provide my unique services to assist with releasing the hurt and pain from individual situations and provide assistance through social media by sharing breathing exercises and YOMA sessions. By providing the services that I created at the beginning of March 2020, I was able to help many people, who had tested positive for the COVID-19 virus, rejuvenate their energy and understand their body. For that, I received thank you letters via email, Instagram DMs, and FB Messenger.

During the COVID-19 pandemic, I asked myself multiple questions such as: How will I get through this? What steps will I take next? Who will I network with? What resources are out there for me? Who do I know that is in my circle? Who can I collaborate with? What actions will allow change to happen? I consistently asked myself those questions and placed them in prayer meditation while preparing the steps that were needed to expand my business and aid in my personal development. In my eyes, that time was a great opportunity to learn new skills, build, and grow in many aspects.

Those questions allowed me to change my circumstances by taking action. God gave me the guidance to remain focused on my many goals and to continue on the right path business-wise. All things happen for a reason and God knew my capabilities in every aspect during the COVID-19 pandemic.

I must state that a very pivotal moment in my life that taught me resilience was losing my late husband who was killed in Iraq when my daughter was three years old. I believe that experience equipped me for the COVID-19 pandemic. The second pivotal moment that equipped me for the pandemic was when I was not able to work for three years due to my injuries. In my eyes, the COVID-19 pandemic itself was the third pivotal moment that taught me life lessons about resilience, new technology, new ways of building my business, and the importance of collaboration. It also allowed me to gain knowledge about additional resources.

Understanding that life can shift right before my eyes allowed me to take a minute to pause, step back and analyze my situation. I've learned that reflecting weekly on every area of life will promote growth, understanding, intuitiveness, vulnerability, transparency, vision, and peace of mind.

The COVID-19 shutdown provided me with the time to tap into the multiple talents God has blessed me with. It also allowed me to gain more knowledge, to network, and to collaborate with amazing individuals. I was able to become a number one bestselling author, create a book business, create various workshops to implement in my business, become an anthologist to create an anthology, and build my talk show and podcast. I was also able to gift my daughter her business; create a journal; launch the nonprofit Humble Haitian Warrior to honor the legacy of my late husband, Sergeant Nelson; provide services for Gold Star families; help clients start their businesses; host various health and wellness events; and become a host, media correspondent, and emcee for numerous conferences.

My most rewarding experience during COVID-19 was at the beginning of May 2020. I received a phone call from ACS (Administration for Children's Services) to provide workshops and classes for the youth. Through working with them, I currently provide services for over 50 group homes and foster homes including those in the LGBTQ community. By word of mouth due to my work ethic, God blessed me to provide services in multiple departments of that organization. God also blessed me with two contracts with the New York

City Police Department and I am in the process of preparing to start another contract with a different company. In 2020, I also began assisting my church with the development of an entrepreneur training program and summits that have been helping others succeed with building their businesses. My business has flourished tremendously. I understand that my drive, impeccable service, and quality customer service is infectious. Each organization that I currently hold contracts with has blessed me, and I have cultivated healthy relationships.

There were multiple practices that helped me during the COVID-19 pandemic. Speaking to God daily allowed my spirit to remain balanced as I assisted other individuals that were experiencing anxiety, depression, hurt, pain, grief, and so much more. Maintaining prayer and meditation, practicing Qigong and Tai Chi, and having faith in the Word of God were also extremely beneficial. The actionable steps that helped me achieve my goals were: being authentic; staying open to new experiences; focusing on my new endeavors; checking in with myself spiritually, mentally, emotionally, and physically; and analyzing my business and its purpose. Networking through social media, participating in various virtual events, collaborating with others, reaching out to those that are in my circle, doing my due diligence with building my business, and not allowing myself to become distracted also helped me to get through the COVID-19 pandemic. God blessed me to cultivate healthy relationships during that time and those relationships are continuously flourishing. Additionally, yoga, kickboxing, and continuing education courses were valuable resources. During the pandemic, I also began attending church services virtually. Being able to accomplish my goals, work on projects, never miss a service, and receive the Word of God brought peace to my heart.

The questions I would ask myself if I were in the same situation today would be *What should I do next?* and *What is God showing me?* After all is said and done, I would take a minute, step back, pause, and practice a meditative prayer. Then I would tell myself, *Let go and let God. Yes, yes.*

If I had a friend that was experiencing that situation, the advice I would give that friend would be: "Trust your relationship with God. If you have any worries or stresses that may be holding on to your mind, body, and spirit, just let them go and let God handle those situations. Understand that you have to put work into trusting God and building a relationship with Him. Take the time to reflect on your self-development and your business development. Also, stay focused and don't allow yourself to become discouraged regardless of distractions.

Life is too short to regret anything. Know that God is preparing you for a fight in life. Be aware of your surroundings by observing the people around you and paying attention to what is happening around you. And when God brings you something in life, don't consult with other people. When God speaks to you, listen. God will give you the approval that is needed to confirm your decisions. Believe with all your heart because all things are possible as long as you believe. Your thoughts are not controlled by your circumstances. God works according to your faith, so tap into your faith and believe beyond all circumstances. Don't let those around you stop you from believing. Fight for your sight in every area of your life, fight for change, and provoke a change in your life by taking action. Faith is your voice. The key is not to let fear hold you back. Understand that when you step out of fear, you will step into grace. Know that there is no growth without pain. And as you build a relationship with God, allow yourself to remain humble.

Negative thoughts will prevent you from growing, so allow the thoughts that go through your mind to be positive. Yes, I know that's easier said than done. The goal is to take care of yourself. Ground your energy and your heart and know that not everybody is meant to walk your path with you.

When your mindset changes, your life will change. You will break the power of offense when you learn how to communicate. Always remain disciplined, stay spiritually balanced, analyze yourself during chaos, provide yourself with self-compassion and self-love, have faith, and be strong. In life, you never know what is next, so always allow yourself to move through life with gratitude and faith."

I hope these words of wisdom touched your heart, mind, body, spirit, and soul and that they allow you to do what needs to be done in your life. Understanding that no one is perfect so show yourself compassion.

Keep Moving Forward

Cindy Brown

Despite the challenges the world faced in 2020, I must say that that year still allowed me to discover a better version of myself. I have always been an optimist. Growing up, I was taught to see the opportunity, not the obstacle. In 2020, I was able to thrive and adjust to the new ways of life and grow through the challenges which taught me some lessons. I will share those lessons and hopefully you will begin to see the best in every situation or obstacle you face. I did not always have this mindset of seeing the opportunity instead of the obstacle, but I am grateful I have learned it.

The little things are what really matter in life. During the COVID-19 pandemic, I was able to build a strong relationship with an older gentleman in my community. Let's call him Mr. B. Mr. B. is 80 years old, tall, dark, and handsome. He shared many stories with me about his past and some of his life's regrets. One of them was not having had a stable life. He was a "rolling stone" as the saying goes which created an unhealthy relationship between himself and his children. "If I ever got to do it again, I would have all my children with one woman to create a stable life and be a better father to my kids. I live a very lonely life, but I am thankful God brought you to assist me," he told me one day.

During the time I spent with Mr. B., I helped him with paying his bills, I took him to the mall to exchange clothes, and I even purchased him a cake for his birthday. I explained to him that we can't live our lives looking backwards. We always have to look ahead to greater things despite the disappointments. That is the only way we will be able to free ourselves and move forward. I also told him that we must always support each other along this journey of life.

Since the time I began speaking to Mr. B., he was able to find love again and embrace the new season of his life. He reconnected with an old friend from 20 years ago and now he has hope for the future. His new beginning allowed him to accept the mistakes of his past, grow into a better person, and realize that life is a journey of peaks and valleys, but in the end we win. His new beginning also allowed me to accept the season I had been in. A season of bringing joy to the life of others and spreading love to each soul. As the saying goes,

"Be kind. Everyone we meet is carrying a heavy burden we cannot see."

Embracing the moment and valuing the people in my life were huge lessons. We often take life and the people in it for granted, but I learned that both are gifts given to us to love and support. We are each made with unique abilities, so we need to value ourselves. And the people in our lives are to be cherished in good times and bad. It was unfortunate that we lost millions of lives due to COVID-19, but those losses allowed us to value life.

Losing someone we love changes our perspective and it allows us to realize that life is very fragile. I lost a very close friend to cancer. I met her at 15 and we remained close until her death in 2020. I was unable to say goodbye to her, but I made sure that I communicated with her as often as possible since I knew that one day she wouldn't be around. Her death allowed me to live every moment of my life from a grateful place and appreciate the little things.

Something as simple as taking a walk in the park allowed me to discover the beauty of nature and the outdoors. I challenged myself to take a hike up Bear Mountain, something I had never done before. It allowed me to challenge myself and step out of my comfort zone. Spending time alone there allowed me to discover my true self, uncover the gift God has placed inside of me, and recognize how precious I am to Him. This is a new beginning for me and for all of us coming out of the pandemic. This time has given birth to my women's empowerment group, Sisters of Excellence, a diverse women's group focused on supporting women of all races in becoming their best selves.

I had to realize that despite being a divorced, black, immigrant, single mother, I was still unconditionally loved by God. I am a masterpiece made in His image for a great purpose—to impact the lives of all with love. Understanding how much God loves me and how valuable I am to Him allowed me to not look for outside validation but to know internally that I am fearfully and wonderfully made. Thinking that I was valuable only because of what I do was a misconception. I am valuable just the way I am, with all of my flaws and my brokenness.

That new revelation allowed me to accept myself and it permitted me to view my past as lessons I had to learn to be empowered for my destiny. It allowed me to look forward and know that all things are possible. Looking forward allowed me to see the future with great possibility, forgetting those things behind and looking for the things ahead. Looking forward has given me great vision for the new gifts—singing, acting, and business acumen—that I have discovered within myself.

My new beginning will allow me to work on the seeds placed inside of me and become my best self. I will be able to build my own world. A world where I will receive an Oscar award, support women globally, and build a business that will assist the less fortunate. I have discovered the power to create the life I want. I am letting the past go and moving forward into a beautiful life of love and self-acceptance. It's a new season and I'm a new me!

We all have the power to look for the positive or negative in every situation. So, moving forward, look for the good. Also, be bold, be confident, be you.

I'm Still Standing

Denise Kennedy

*You can't really speak to something if your heart
has not experienced it, otherwise you're just a
make-up artist.*

I started to write this chapter on an awful COVID
morning, as the broken and shadeless lamp on my
nightstand flickered on and off. I didn't know if it
would stay on or shut off, what I would do, what
I would say, or where I would go. It was a faceless
day as I thought about all the senseless lives lost.

I am a strong, black, wonderfully made woman born of a strong, black, wonderfully made
woman. I am an entrepreneur and an inspired novice poet. This is my story, and I am sticking to it.
Because my dot sits on the "S" for sincerity and
dependability, and sometimes touches on enthusi-
asm, my inherent personality allows me to develop
and maintain long-term relationships. No matter
what kind—work, personal, church, real estate,
matrimonial—I boast about the longevity of my
relationships. But oh, I got the surprise of my life

on that matrimonial part. I did not get the chance to live my "happily ever after" as I now find myself alone, without a spouse. I am "the big D"—D I V O R C E D (um, that's the first time I've written that dirty eight letter word).

Let me tell you what happened to me, you are not going to believe this. Just as COVID-19 was beginning to manifest itself (rearing its ugly, venomous, Medusa-like head), I received the news. I was at home just chilling when there was a knock at the door. I asked, "Who is it?" The deep, frightened voice on the other side of the door said, "Package for Mrs. Kennedy." I questioned myself, *Mrs. Kennedy?* When I opened the door, the reedy dude gave me an envelope. If you had seen the smirk on his face, you would have smacked him. As I took the envelope and closed the door, I suspiciously stared at the package then opened it. The only word that stood out on the enclosed piece of paper was that dirty eight-letter word, D I V O R C E D. It jumped out at me in 3D. It was confirmed, yep it was final. I was officially D I V O R C E D.

After what seemed like an eternity, I caught my breath. But I felt like my feet were stuck in aggregates of sand and gravel. I was afraid and I realized that I was going to be in the COVID-19 pandemic by myself due to those eight letters of permanent separation. To tell you the truth, after feeling betrayed, I just wanted my marriage to be over. So no, I did not contest the divorce. I just let him leave. If he could do this to me after all of the years we were together, he nor my entitlements were worth fighting for or losing my peace of mind over. I chose me. And although keeping my head above water was a challenge every single day, I survived and I'm still standing. 1 Corinthians 7:15 ERV reads: "But if the husband or wife who is not a believer decides to leave, let them leave. When this happens, the brother or sister in Christ is free. God chose you to have a life of peace."

Although I have a full-time job with benefits, that wasn't enough. My life-changing event opened my eyes and made me step up my real estate game. I am a sole proprietor, a licensed real estate sales-person, an SRS (seller representative specialist) designate, and a notary public with an awesome franchised real estate firm and an amazing associ-ate broker. I had to refocus my attention, time, and energy on getting more listings, getting more cli-ents to the closing table, and taking as many con-tinuing education classes as possible so that I could get as many real estate designations as possible just to stay in the game. It wasn't easy. In fact, it was a challenge trying to make two short ends meet giv-en my situation and the CDC guidelines for busi-nesses due to COVID-19. My girlfriend would say to me, "You stay in the streets, what didn't you do today?" She was absolutely right. I went into work early, I stayed late, I worked from home, and I worked on Saturdays and Sundays (after church of course). As a licensed real estate salesperson, I'll relocate you, I'll help you buy a home, and I'll sell your house in a Nueva York minute. You want to downsize? Call me! You want to upsize? Call me! First time homebuyers, call me! Renters, call me! About to go into foreclosure, call a sister!

I tried to keep up with my financial responsibilities, but I had to borrow money from Peter to pay Paul to keep the bill collectors from calling my cell phone, my home, and my job. They would call and say, "Hello, is this Mrs. Kennedy? Your rent is past due." I would respond, "No, there's a moratorium." Click! "Hello, is this Mrs. Kennedy? Did you know that your credit score has just dropped from a 720 to a 550?" I would respond, "I wish I had $550 right now." Click! "Hello, is this Mrs. Kenn– ?" "No." Click! Needless to say, I still had to figure out how I was going to pay the rent, car payment, car insurance, groceries, life insurance, utilities, credit cards, phone bill, medical bills, dental bills, and vision bills. They seemed to never stop coming. Pampering myself at the salon and getting a manicure or pedicure were now a luxury. I even considered filing for bankruptcy.

Mr. Dunbar talked about wearing a mask to hide your emotions. Believe me when I tell you that I did not look like what I was going through. I kept myself together. I surely did wear a mask, but not just to hide my emotions of despair and abandonment. I wore an actual mask, a protective covering, because I was also afraid that just a droplet or molecule of the COVID-19 virus might attack my eyes or nostrils or some exposed part of my body and I would have to die alone, without my husband by my side.

I know your pain. The eyes are the soul of the broken heart. I understand those unrelenting tears cried all night, out of sight from the world. I've been there too. I would often ask myself questions like, *How did I get here? When did I get here? How did I let this happen to me at this age and at this time in my life? What did I do so wrong that I deserve to be in this place?* As the divorce rate was skyrocketing, COVID-19 was leaving its trail of broken families, including mine. What happened to my marriage vows—in sickness and in health… till death do us part? I guess the pandemic got to us first. I decided that I must keep moving forward. I could not stay in that dark place! I could not make it my home! I started repeating this affirmation to myself every day: *This is not my home and I am coming out! It's a new day. My day!*

As I started my day each morning, I woke up with a praise in my mouth. I thanked God for allowing me to see another day, to be able to breathe, to talk, to walk, to do things for myself, and to survive. Every day my sisters in Christ (I'll call them The Five Prayer Warriors) and I would have a group text of Scriptures, prayers, gospel songs, uplifting quotes, laughter, and encouragement. I prayed without ceasing with Pastor B. and took communion every first Sunday to keep from losing myself and to maintain my sanity.

When I finally got my caramel-colored skin back, I started fighting my way forward to the new me. After some soul searching, I found that even though I was strong, I had become complacent. That's when I realized that I needed to make a change in my life. I had to become forceful, bold, and resilient.

Someone once told me that I always had some harebrained scheme I was working on. In reality, it was my creative entrepreneurship evolving. I welcomed the opportunity to be a co-author in this book. I wanted to tell my story and share my pain through the poetry I wrote during the healing process; thereby, hopefully helping someone else through their healing process. This opportunity to be a co-author, my divorce, and thus this chapter has awakened me.

"After the Divorce, I Woke Up"

After the divorce, I woke up from my sleep and slumber

As apathy had taken me over, under

Without even realizing that I was asleep

So deep, the darkness so black I couldn't even see

See you, looking at me, me looking at you

Blinded by contorted emotions, reading your thoughts in braille

Oh but I woke up after the divorce

Wake up! I know who I am… I am awake!

I'm Still Standing

As I hit the restart button as the CEO of Pocket of Hope, a Christian towel and clothing company, I realize that I now have the time to focus on my company and to jumpstart it again. I now get to put the focus on myself—to do what Denise wants to do, when Denise wants to do it, and how Denise wants to do it. I started my company in 2014 and although I had to put it on the back burner for a little while, it is now time to introduce my passion to the world. When I look at my bathroom and kitchen towel line, chills run up and down my spine. Since its inception, Pocket of Hope has evolved from just an idea into an amazing Christian line. I was inspired to start my business because I wanted to give hope and encouragement to those who have life-threating illness. They can use my line of bath towels to wrap themselves in security, hope, and peace of mind. I didn't realize until 2020 that I too would need my own line for encouragement and to help me move forward.

In closing, I want you to be encouraged and speak over yourself. Put on your own oxygen mask before you try to put on someone else's. In layman's terms: fix yourself before you try to fix someone else. I am somebody and you are too. Don't make misery your home and don't let anyone steal your joy. Repeat after me: "This is not my home. I am coming out! It's a new day, my day!" As Psalm 27:5 NKJV says, "For in the time of trouble He shall hide me in his pavilion; In the secret place of his tabernacle He shall hide me; He shall set me high upon a rock."

As for the pandemic, I don't really believe that things will ever go back to "normal" or business as usual. However, I do believe that we are like babies who have to learn how to walk and talk again. We must also pray always and learn the new ways of working and living in this environment. If you really think about it, everyone in this world is now connected by one common dominator—COVID-19.

We have all been touched by it in some way. Maybe it was the loss of a dear family member who was the glue that held the family and everything else together, friends who listened to you when no one else would and with whom you could share your deepest intimate thoughts and they would tell you "no" for your own good when you wanted them to tell you "yes" for your own pleasure, coworkers who covered for you when you came in late or ate someone's else lunch from the fridge, or church members who sang that song that you loved so much or preached about Shadrach, Meshach and Abednego. Believe it or not, we are all connected in some shape or form by COVID-19. The pandemic is real, and we all have a story to tell.

"The Healing Process"

Can you see what I see far, far away in the desert sand uncountable

A place where he has hidden me in the shadows of self

Hiding my beautifully freckled face and my broken heart shattered into pieces of a puzzle

My voice gives me away

Can't hear, touch or see my sensual smile

Behind a mountain of pain that I thought no one could sense but me

Trying to remove those concrete boots I've obliviously crocheted for myself

Stuck for what seemed like an eternity

A holding pattern

He had me, me had he

Wait! Rewind, disconnect and restart The Healing Process

No more dwelling on the past in self-pity, Waddling like a pig in quicksand

No more crying and whimpering like a newborn baby without his mother's milk

No more holding onto those feelings of pastel colors of bright pink, yellow and mint green turned into darkness

Wait! Rewind, disconnect and restart The Healing Process

Acceptance and Hope, the last stages

I want to thank God for His continuous covering and His grace and mercies. I also want to thank Him for my sanity, peace that surpasses all understanding, and this opportunity to tell my story. He is a way maker. I also want to thank my mom Kathryn, my sister Audrey, and my brother Norman for being supportive of me and for all of their words of encouragement. I would like to especially thank the two men in my life who are the reasons my heart beats—my sons Paul and Darryl. Thank you both for loving me unconditionally and for always treating me with respect like a queen. I love you all.

Pushing Through the Test During COVID

Kelvin Weathers

It is a privilege and an honor to be connected with this project. My name is Kelvin Weathers. I am an African American male who has been married for eight years. I have resided in Houston, Texas, pretty much all of my life and I am the oldest of five children. I have been in the sales field for the past 16 years and I am also a public speaker.

The year 2020 was very difficult and extremely challenging. I now want to give just a bit of what may be hopeful reflections from my journey during that time and season. As I began 2020, I was full of excitement and I had great expectations; I had a really good feeling about that year. However, in the middle of that year, I faced a set of unfortunate setbacks that were not related to the COVID-19 pandemic. In addition to all that I do, I am an itinerant minister who preaches almost weekly, but because of COVID-19 and some churches transitioning to virtual worship services, many of my preaching assignments were canceled. I also worked part-time as a rideshare driver for Lyft.

I had left a job in collections many months earlier and preaching along with being a rideshare driver were my main sources of income. I had previously driven for Uber for two years before being disallowed because of a background check issue. I began working for Lyft in June of 2019. I decided to continue to work as a Lyft driver during COVID-19 in spite of the risk and possible safety hazard. I felt that I could still drive safely and securely. I drove for Lyft until April 26, 2020. At that time, I had close to a five-star rating and had driven almost 3,000 passengers.

On April 26, 2020, I attempted to check into the Lyft app as usual, but I was not allowed to. It stated that there was an issue with my background check. The background check I had undergone and passed when I was accepted as a Lyft driver. I'd been accepted twice and worked for them but now I was being rejected? I'd had no issues with my background since becoming a driver. I'd even received a Lyft jacket free of charge for performing 1,000 rides and doing an exceptional job as a driver with no incidents or driving complaints. Yet because of a conviction from almost nine years prior that was attached to my background, I was fired.

Faced with challenges from my past and the present, what was I to do? Thoughts of doubt and depression started to creep into my mind almost daily. I'm a black male, we were in a pandemic, there was social unrest all around, and I was not working. I'm a competitive person by nature and I started to feel a sense of dejection and trouble in my spirit. How was I going to pay the bills? I could not be taken out and defeated permanently by my circumstances. I believed I could still win and thrive; yet, the odds almost seemed insurmountable. But with the faith I had in God, who has never disappointed or left me, I still believed in a better day. I asked Him to help me deal with my dilemma, I asked my family to support me, and I asked my wife to stand by me. Since March 2019, I had only been working as a gig share driver. I was forced to file for unemployment benefits in May 2020.

Filing for unemployment was not what I wanted to do. I enjoyed serving and interacting with passengers and working as a Lyft driver. I did not want to live on unemployment benefits or any type of government assistance. I was faced with having to adapt to being on unemployment. For much of my time as a husband, I had been the sole breadwinner in my home. Now, I was out of many preaching assignments and unable to drive. What would I do to make money?

I decided to continue to pursue my search for employment. I was not going to let what people considered my shameful past continue to define my future. I believe as Charles Swindoll states: "Life is 10% what happens to me and 90% of how I react to it." I was determined to not let my setback become a permanent roadblock and stop me from my destiny. So, since I'm also a licensed life insurance agent, I decided to focus more on that. My life insurance sales started to pick up slowly during the COVID-19 pandemic. Also, I decided on May 3, 2020, to start using FB Live to give messages of encouragement and inspiration weekly. That was a collaborative effort with other ministers who would use the platform for what would be deemed "Unity Sunday" on the first Sunday of each month. I was unsure and anxious about using FB Live and other platforms without a live audience to speak in front of. I had never done so before May of 2020. The weekly broadcasts I had done had been well received. Other ministers encouraged me to use social media platforms to speak each week. One day as I was perusing Facebook, I saw a sponsored ad from "Mike the Motivator" Nelson, a speaker in the education market and an education consultant.

I was also able to have a one-on-one session with him about speaking in the education market (middle schools, high schools, and colleges) to students. Since I started preaching, I have always believed that I am gifted to speak to and impact audiences. Seeing "Mike the Motivator" Nelson, Jeremy Anderson, Eric Thomas, and others lit a fire in me to speak to different audiences. I was impressed with Les Brown and other speakers over the years but I never thought about myself being a full-time transformational motivational speaker.

Proverbs 18:16 says, "A man's gift maketh room for him, and bringeth him before great men." I was able to create a profile on SpeakerHub, a website that showcases speakers, and I started to speak outside of churches to other organizations such as the Rochester Urban League. I also spoke during some virtual church sermons in the summer of 2020, which includes the nearly one thousand member Fifth Ward Church of Christ at which I spoke twice. I preached on a couple of occasions in person and spoke at the Interrupt Racism Summit in October 2020.

In May 2020, I was offered a position to work from home with Relia Home Buyers. The pay structure of the position was changed to commission after I accepted the role. So, I was without stable income once again. A couple of months later, I received a message through LinkedIn from a corporate recruiter for HomeAdvisor. I interviewed with the recruiter and he was impressed with my skill set and asked me to continue in the process and have a second interview. I interviewed with the recruiter and a manager the next day, then I was given an employment offer.

In early August 2020, I started working as a sales consultant for HomeAdvisor. My employment included a six-week training program. I graduated early from training and received an early graduation bonus on September 11, 2020.

We were in a time of social unrest, economic uncertainty, racial tension, and a contentious presidential election, but I believed we could still thrive. My story is a testament to the fact that getting knocked down is not the challenge. The bigger issue is whether you stay down or not. I have been blessed more than I deserve to be. In spite of my past, I'm still able to succeed. The mistakes I made and the lessons I learned during the pandemic made me a better man, a better husband, a better brother, and a better son.

How can we still thrive during a pandemic and times of turmoil? I believe our thoughts are key to maintaining our sanity and overcoming the challenges this life puts before us. Persistent negative thoughts can cripple us and impede our future. As James Allen said, "You are today where your thoughts have brought you; you will be tomorrow where your thoughts take you." We can all overcome.

"Finally, brothers, whatever is true, whatever is honorable, whatever is just, whatever is pure, whatever is lovely, whatever is commendable, if there is any excellence, if there is anything worthy of praise, think about these things."—Philippians 4:8. Also, what we say to and about ourselves and the people we associate with is key to us achieving our goals in troubled times. "As iron sharpens iron, so one person sharpens another."—Proverbs 27:17.

I would like to share why I have not passed the recent background checks and why they were a barrier to some opportunities in my life. On Tuesday evening, September 28, 2010, I went to a gospel revival meeting at a church. A revival is a meeting where people come together with other Christians to get closer to God and refresh themselves. I drove down Highway 288 South to Moore Avenue Church of Christ in Bay City, Texas. I left the meeting a few minutes early, around 8:30 p.m., once the sermon had concluded. It was my first time in Bay City and I was not familiar with the area. I got lost going back to Highway 288 on my way home, so I stopped at a local store to ask how I could get back to Houston. I was told to go West from the area I was in, then I would get to Highway 59 and I could go to Houston from there. I drove from the store and went West on 59–Sugar Land/Richmond.

Since I really didn't know the area well, I drove cautiously as not to get lost again. As I was driving, with my seat belt on and obeying the law, I heard a siren but didn't know where it was coming from. Then, I heard someone saying, "Pull over," via megaphone. I wasn't told or didn't hear where to pull over, so I pulled over to the right shoulder and stopped. I was immediately approached in a hostile manner. I heard the gentleman say, "What's wrong with you? Do you have a problem?" He seemed extremely upset and irritated with me. He came up to my passenger side window. I was a little surprised because that was my first time in that type of situation. He then said, "Put the window down." I could not get it down fast enough for him. I was never told why I was being stopped, instead he said, "Give me your license and insurance, and get out of the car." I reached over to get the information from the glove compartment then heard him say, "Or I will yank you out of the car." He then came to the driver's side and opened the door.

He proceeded to attempt to pull me out of the car by grabbing me by my neck and shoulders while I asked, "Why am I being stopped?" He said, "You're being arrested for disobeying a peace officer. You were speeding." He again grabbed me and pulled on me to get me out of the car. My shirt was torn on my right side at that point. I said, "You're abusing me." His hat came off. I said, "I'm a minister."

I felt like I was being treated like an animal, so I closed the door, started the vehicle, and proceeded to leave. I drove in the same lane on the freeway for about 10-15 minutes. I was not going at a high rate of speed. Then I saw a blockade in the center of the freeway with officers and I stopped the car, got on the ground, and they arrested me.

Being on the ground then, and seeing where I am today, reminds me that even though you make mistakes and fall, you can get back up. You can rise from the ashes. Whether it's past COVID, or after a failure, you can get back up.

How to Navigate Life's Challenges in Times of Crisis

Nkechi Ogbodo

"Life is what happens while you are busy making other plans."
—John Lennon

The COVID-19 pandemic came at a time when everyone least expected it. We were all forced to adapt and make something out of those circumstances. Now, we are all a part of the "new normal." Many challenges have come up along the path of this new normal. Some people have thrived since the onset of the pandemic, while others have not coped well. But how do you navigate the challenges that this life brings so that you can forge ahead and make something of it?

My immediate concern about the pandemic (at the onset) was not immediately the loss of income, as I (like many others) thought we would be back on the streets in no time. It was the mystery surrounding the reality that shook the world so rudely. It was the helplessness of humanity in the face of a raging disease. It was the uncertainty that greeted our tomorrows (health wise) that was my immediate concern at the onset of COVID-19. It was when the pandemic raged on, when our movements became more locked and economic activities under lock and key, that the next immediate concern of mine centered on the uncertainty of one's economic survival. I mean, the world had become extremely sick, and economic activities the world over were at a melting point.

Two major events played a significant role in helping me to navigate the COVID-19 pandemic and other obstacles that I have faced. The first major event was leaving Nigeria. For many girls, growing up in Nigeria was a daunting experience due to cultural impediments. At an early age, I was determined to leave Nigeria and leaving gave me a sense of courage and determination. I was on my own and I had no choice but to thrive so that I could make my parents proud. Still, nothing prepared me for the unknown and what was to come next. The second major event was the kidnapping of my mother. On June 14, 2011, my world was shattered when I received a phone call from Nigeria that my mother was kidnapped by unknown gunmen. That experience was traumatic not only for my mom but for my entire family. My mom was taken for eight weeks and my family was told to pay a ransom by the gunmen for her release. After her release, I embarked on a mission to make a difference in the lives of others.

I founded the nonprofit organization, Kechie's Project Inc., to help address challenges women and girls are facing in Nigeria and Africa as a whole. Instead of seeing my mom as a victim, the situation gave me the courage to stand up for the voiceless—to educate, mentor, and be a voice to girls in underserved communities in Nigeria. My mom now has a voice through me. Though my mother's rights were violated, I am using that adversity to help her and support many unknowns who have been equally violated.

There is no time like the present to begin taking control of what is occurring in your life. Now is the time to set goals, strategize, and forge ahead despite the obstacles that may present themselves. In March 2020, I was one of the style advisors that were furloughed for almost five months. When I was called back in the middle of June, pandemic or not, I was determined to achieve my goal of over one million dollars in sales. Today, I am one of the few style advisors at Saks Fifth Avenue that achieved that goal in those challenging times.

How Do I Keep Forging Ahead?

COVID-19 came and so did the very unexpected lockdown. Many of us had never been in such a situation. We had always had the freedom to move around as we desired. Instead, businesses were closed, schools were shut down, many social activities were canceled, and travel was restricted. In that situation, anyone's mental health would be affected. Anxiety, depression, and even suicidal attempts can surface, especially when job loss, a downturn in the economy, adjustments in schooling, or a change in your financial situation arises. The impact that the COVID-19 pandemic had on people of color and other minorities as well as the elderly was greater than for others.

Almost one year into the pandemic, some cities and countries re-entered lockdown. Because the pandemic was something that was unexpected, we were all unsure how to navigate it. Now that we know how to adjust and what to anticipate, we can look at the pandemic and other challenges in a more positive light and be more focused. During the pandemic, doing things such as monitoring my anxiety and practicing mindfulness worked for me. I started by taking note of my environment at work. I assessed how I was feeling and observed how others around me felt. The uncertainty of the pandemic resulted in much discomfort, causing many people to think and act in ways that were not normal.

Life in a pandemic is hard, especially when our emotions get involved. But ultimately, we get to choose our mindset. For me, developing and having a growth mindset helped me to cope. The growth mindset is all about self-improvement. You can read and research anything you want to know more about and take on a different, more positive approach to life despite the odds.

Take Care of Yourself

Many of us are facing challenges that have caused us to become incredibly stressed. Many times, we stress because we are trying to help others before we even help ourselves. There is a saying, "You cannot pour from an empty cup" and truer words have never been spoken.

You have your family to take care of, bills to pay, and just life in general to navigate. So, how do we balance it all while keeping it together?

1. **Take breaks and unwind.** You can do this by moving your body (i.e., doing yoga), listening to your favorite music, or kicking back and indulging in your favorite hobby. Give yourself permission to not be perfect. Whatever is happening, always remember that you are doing your best.

2. **Treat and pamper yourself from time to time.** Go ahead, you deserve it.

3. **Get rest.** Nothing can replace or substitute for rest. Listen to your body and rest when you need to. We may feel the need to do more, especially in a situation such as a pandemic, but burnout is real. Rest comes in to help rejuvenate and heal our bodies.

4. **Limit your news consumption.** It is good for us to stay abreast of what is happening around us but sometimes we can take in too much and suffer from information overload, which can negatively impact our mental health and mood. Therefore, it is important for you to do all things in moderation.

5. **Seek support if you need it.** We cannot go it alone. Keep in contact with your friends and family. You can use technology in a positive way to help you stay connected. If you do not think that you have a support system, seek professional help to guide you.

6. **Develop and stick to a routine.** Create a routine that you like and stick to it. A routine will help keep your mind occupied and at ease. It may also help you to make more sound decisions.

7. **Focus on the positive.** Put your focus on things that you can control. If you cannot readily do

anything about it, then don't keep it on your mind.

8. **Acknowledge your feelings and allow yourself to experience them.** This is advice that you would not normally hear, but the only way to really confront your negative feelings is to name them and then work your way through them. It is also important to note that there is no right or wrong way to feel about what you are experiencing. Feel how you feel then work your way through to a more positive perspective.

9. **Practice gratitude.** Take the time out to be grateful, even if it's just for one thing. When you practice gratitude, it can shift your focus from what you don't have to what you do have.

10. **Be kind to yourself.** If you do not feel like doing anything today, that's perfectly fine. Do not be the negative voice in your head. Be proud of what you have achieved so far and be optimistic about what the future holds.

Self-care is one of the first steps we should take while navigating life's challenges and preparing to forge ahead.

Make Your Plans... Here are Some Suggestions

Hope has not been lost. Since the onset of the COVID-19 pandemic, we have learned the importance of planning. We adapted to what is now the new normal. Everything went digital and we simply had to just go with the flow. Countless families of color and other minorities have had it particularly hard. For many, their household income became non-existent, while others had to pivot and make life and career changes on the spot.

Numerous people are now refusing to let COVID-19 stop them from pursuing their dreams. There has been a tremendous spike in enrollment to online courses as well as in the emergence of e-commerce businesses.

So, yes, you should still make your plans and forge ahead, pandemic or no pandemic. If your plans cannot be executed right away, find creative avenues to begin putting things into place. Educating yourself on things that are of interest to you can be the first step. The more you know, the better you will be. However, do not limit your education to only the subjects that entertain you. Spend less time on social media and things that do not help you reach your purpose. You can read inspirational books to learn about how others navigated through their ups and downs to be where they are today. Manage your time wisely.

After making your big plans, you should conquer them in small bite-sized pieces. Do not try to bite off more than you can chew. That is a sure recipe for burnout, stress, and disaster. Pick one thing to do, focus on it, and get to work. When you are done with that one thing, you can move on to the next thing.

In all that you have set out to pursue, do not forget to celebrate your small wins. Every hurdle that you get over will take you one step closer to your ultimate goal. Pat yourself on the back, take a step back to briefly look at what you have accomplished, then take a deep breath and get going again.

Be sure to also remember why you started. What is your why? Why do you want this thing so badly? Envision the end result and never lose sight of it. When you feel like you have come to a crossroads and can't find a reason to carry on, just remember your why.

Forging Ahead

In times of crisis like we experienced with the COVID-19 pandemic, it is not easy to ignore the realities of the situation in hopes of a bright future. Keep an open mind and expect difficulties to come, but at the same time do not lose hope that things will get better.

Life is a journey, and it does not stop for us when we want a break. The solution? We must simply keep moving forward. No matter how slow you go, every step will count because you are one step closer to your goals than you were before.

Another important element in forging ahead is learning how to enjoy the journey. See life for what it is and accept it, but do not forget to enjoy it as you go along. The saying goes, "Stop and smell the roses," and that is exactly what enjoying the journey means.

When you can overcome your challenges, it creates a sense of internal pride and joy. On the flip side of overcoming your challenges there will be roadblocks. When you face them, be sure not to dwell on them. Instead, focus on possible solutions that will help to propel you forward. Remember that overcoming challenges is also a part of enjoying the journey.

Forging ahead simply means that you are willing to take the lead as your life's journey progresses. Some of us may have to dig deep to carry on, but we must muster up the strength and get going. If we prepare now, we will be well on our way when the time of crisis ends.

Be Encouraged

Motivation is a powerful tool. It is something that indeed helps us to keep on keeping on. Take things a day at a time and do not be consumed by what you see in the media, especially on social media. Limit your daily consumption if things get too overwhelming. You can also choose to follow people and pages that are uplifting and those that push positivity. There are also many social media pages that constantly produce positive quotes and encouraging messages, and mental health pages that give tips on how to handle anxiety and deal with depression. In fact, there is a whole world of positivity, inspiration, and motivation out there if we look in the right places. So, keep building your network and stay abreast of what is happening in the spaces that interest you. There are also mountains of materials in circulation that speak about wellness and mindfulness. Your body is indeed a temple and your mind is sacred, so you must seek to water it daily with positivity, affirmations, and love.

In this season of your life, you might even want to reignite some passions that you previously put on the back burner. Did you like playing the piano? Were you good at chess? Or better yet, were you a star football or soccer player? Sometimes it is a good thing to look back. In this instance, you will be looking back and remembering what you were good at so that you can make plans to catch up on what you were missing out on.

Where Do We Go from Here?

Being Black or any other minority during the COVID-19 pandemic had its challenges. There were disadvantages in accessing education, food, and even health care. But do not lose hope! The possibility of change still exists. It may be difficult, but the change can begin with us.

We can forge ahead and keep encouraging ourselves, our children, and others who we love. Ambition and resilience run through the veins of many of our people and we will not stand by and be defeated. There are many of us who remain optimistic despite challenges because we are very much aware that this too shall pass.

One of the biggest setbacks of our time is that people are afraid to ask for help, but we must never be afraid to ask for help if we need it. There is a constant desire to feel and be independent. While that is important, there are times when we simply cannot do things alone. No man is an island and if we continue with the do-it-yourself attitude, especially in challenging times, the possibility of failure and mistakes and even loneliness are left out in the open just waiting to happen.

Build or join a community of like-minded people who can offer an ear or lend support in other ways. You may be surprised just how beneficial that proves to be.

We Shall Overcome

Life comes down to this: keep your emotions in check, take care of yourself first and then those around you, continue to make plans and put things into place, keep forging ahead, and remain encouraged and optimistic through it all.

We are living in unprecedented times and nothing is certain. If you are only able to do one thing, I encourage you to bank on yourself and never lose sight of your goals. Keep forging ahead and keep taking those steps, no matter how small or slow. Take your time and put things into perspective. You are right where you need to be. The same body, brain, and abilities that got you this far are more than capable of helping you to keep going. Look at difficult and challenging times as things that build your strength and fortitude. You can learn from every setback, making you more experienced and more prepared to take on and face other challenges.

Perspective is everything. It can either make or break us. So, keep your eyes on the prize and things will fall into place. Do your best in everything. You've got this!

Freedom

Michelle Richburg

My name is Michelle A. Amos-Richburg and I am driven by the pursuit of freedom! Freedom? "But we have been free for so long," you say. When I think about what financial literacy means to me, the word that comes to mind is freedom. Led by my faith, this journey has not been an easy one. I don't claim to have a more painful story than anybody else but my pain, my story, and my struggles have all brought me to this exact point in my life. I can now look at my God and say, "Thank you, Lord, for all that you have done for me."

I cannot begin to talk about my journey without first saying that if it were not for my faith, I do not know how I would have made it through 2020. That year was shaping up to be one of my best professional and personal years ever, then boom... a pandemic hit, social unrest was at an all-time high triggered by the senseless murders of George Floyd and Breonna Taylor, and to bring it all home my dear father who I love more than words can describe passed away alone due to the restrictions of COVID-19. So again, I say freedom. Freedom from worry. Freedom from the pains of yesterday. Freedom of choice to live a blessed life on our own terms. Financial freedom!

Let me start from the beginning of my story. Growing up, I was always impressed with my grandmother's independence. Watching the choices she made as a black woman is the reason I chose the financial sector as my path to independence. I was fascinated with the power of the almighty dollar, good credit, and the genius of smart investments and long-term planning. All of that spelled freedom to me as I watched so many people of color struggle to get off of the hamster wheel of debt. I do not believe that one finds happiness in money, but there is a freedom of choice and a multitude of options that money affords you. It is no secret that one of the numerous stressors in life is money as without it many people wonder how they will survive. Having spent my entire life inside of the financial sector while raising my son as a single black mom, I know all too well what that stress looks and feels like. I needed to be an example to my son that regardless of our circumstances, we could still be free to be what we wanted on our own terms. Having spent over 30 years advising and educating people on the importance of financial literacy (explaining why paying your taxes is important and why saving for a rainy day is more than just some kind words uttered to you by your grandparents) saving and having an emergency fund is even more important today as we recently endured the worst pandemic this country has seen since the Great Depression.

"Decide. Commit. Act. Succeed. Repeat."

—Tim Grover, *Relentless*

For over 30 years, I developed a niche in the financial services industry as a "banker to the stars." I am proud to say that I have built a long, trustworthy relationship servicing high profile clients from all walks of entertainment to professional athletes and business leaders. My skills range from banking, royalty and contract review, auditing and analysis, forecasting, and risk management to investment consulting. I truly believe that my career path was decided at a very young age under the wise guidance of my grandmother. I watched her buy four houses (no mortgages ever) with money she saved from her domestic worker's salary. She had no formal education. In fact, the last grade she completed was the ninth grade. My grandmother was my first superhero! The very foundation that my career is built on stems from the examples that were instilled in me by her, the matriarch of our family.

Decide. Commit. Act. Succeed. Repeat!

As I continued to rise through the ranks at different financial institutions such as Chase, National Westminster, Fleet Bank (currently Bank of America), and Citibank, just to name a few, it became apparent to me that to truly have the impact that I wanted to have and to leave a legacy for my son, I would have to venture out on my own. My decision, however, was not merely of my own doing but largely the result of what I would describe as a forced pivot.

Pivot is probably the word that will describe a lot of people's professional decisions in 2020 due to layoffs, business closures, and the financial comfort being ripped from underneath many of us as a result of the pandemic. My forced pivot came in 2011 as a result of me being fired from my job as senior vice-president of private clients. I was forced to reinvent myself. While I did have some financial cushion, as a single mom a few months hardly cuts it.

After creating financial roadmaps and solutions for thousands of clients and several banks throughout the years, I realized my superpower was in my ability to take seemingly complex financial problems and simplify them for my clients. I have always felt that we should never make anyone feel uncomfortable or inadequate when discussing money, especially their own. I found that most business managers lack the skills necessary to communicate with their clients in a way that creates a collaborative environment for proper and effective financial planning.

I decided to establish Richburg Enterprises, LLC in 2014 partly out of the frustration I experienced while witnessing the mishandling of several of my clients. I would often see gross negligence or just pure disregard for how the client and their money was treated at the financial institution. Sometimes, lack of communication or real transparency was what led to poor financial outcomes that in most cases could have been avoided. Where was the caring? Where were the financial experts that viewed their clients as real partners building empires and not transactional objects to make a commission off of?

"History is not the past. It is the present."

—James Baldwin

In 1995, a young Michelle Richburg was stranded! My son's father and I shared one car at the time and while there was no immediate danger in that very moment, I felt helpless. Something as simple as wanting to run to the grocery store seemed like an impossible feat. Instead of him dropping everything and coming to bring me the car or better yet coming to take care of me, he left me to fend for myself. Looking back, experiences like that are one of the many reasons why I have always stressed the importance of financial freedom. Would my grandmother ever let a man leave her stranded? How did I allow myself to be in this place?

While I felt very confident in my professional journey, even though it was still just beginning, I had not claimed that same freedom in my personal life. It is very important that we do not separate the two. I have learned over the years that how you do one thing speaks volumes to how you do everything else. I was starting on a path of professional excellence but had not created the same standards and goals in my personal life. How did I expect to have one without the other?

That realization in 1995 changed me and brings me to the present day as many of us are trying to figure out how to survive and pivot during these trying times. As a small double minority business owner, I am constantly assessing my business and that of my clients. Are we prepared for the worst? I have made it a life practice since that faithful day in 1995 to keep a six-month reserve of savings no matter what. You never know when a global pandemic will hit or when your life will turn upside down. The emotional stress of life's events is enough, why add financial pressure to the list?

I mentioned earlier that I lost my father, but not due to COVID-19. However, because we were in a pandemic, it made simple things like visiting him in the hospital or having a normal funeral service impossible. The emotional toll was truly exhausting but having my affairs in order allowed me the room and space to grieve unencumbered.

"Rather than crying about water being wet, we choose to teach our young men and women how to swim."

—Jonathan Walton

That quote echoes my purpose—to not only teach my son how to swim but my clients, friends, and family as well. We should not allow ourselves to become financially stuck. We must not carry such heavy financial burdens that it makes it impossible to pivot when life happens because one thing is for sure, life will happen, it always does!

Do not let 2020 have been for naught, let it have been a lesson. Do not continue through life thinking that the world will go back to what you knew it to be before the COVID-19 pandemic. God does not make mistakes or look backwards; He only looks forward. The world has changed and hopefully our priorities have changed too. I hope that now more than ever we have learned the importance of mental and physical health and planning for the future. We should not need a global pandemic to scare us straight. If we can live by faith and freedom, we can accomplish all things!

I hope that my honesty inspires you and makes it clear that despite the obstacles you face, big or small, nothing is impossible. I write so that we may see that there is no success without failure. No matter what path you choose, set your intention on greatness and your sights on the sky above because up is the only direction we should be striving for. As a black woman, I feel that it is my duty to pass along whatever knowledge I have gained through all of my trials. I want my legacy to be that I helped to remove the stigma that artists, creatives, and athletes are incapable of grasping the notion of smart financial planning at a young age. Too often, we are led to believe that they must hit the bottom before they get on the right track, but we have many examples (i.e., Oprah, LeBron James, Venus and Serena Williams, and Beyoncé) that prove you can have it all!

I will leave you with this Bible verse, Psalm 27:1, that will always be my guiding principle: "The Lord is my light and my salvation- whom shall I fear? The Lord is the stronghold of my life- of whom shall I be afraid?"

About the Authors

PK Kersey has been married for over 29 years to his wife Keenya. He is the father of twin boys, Kell and Kye. PK was an employee for the New York State Department of Motor Vehicles for over 24 years, where he progressed to office manager. PK left the DMV to form his nonprofit, further his desire to assist men in obtaining work, and aid high school students in attending prom and graduation while looking sharp in professional attire. Since its inception, That Suits You has assisted over 9,000 individuals in obtaining the clothing, information, and motivation needed to go to the next level in their lives.

PK is also the author of the bestselling series, Suited for Success, which includes stories written by black men to inspire the next generation, as well as the co-author of the children's book *That Suits You, Kid!*

Learn more at
www.thatsuitsyou.org

Nakita Vanstory, a proud native of Greensboro, North Carolina, has resided in New York City for over 25 years. She personifies professionalism, unbridled passion, a resilient overcomer, and what it means to go above and beyond. Nakita has an army to attest to her influence in their lives. As a senior-level workforce development leader, she has over 20 years of experience designing job readiness content, workplace credentialing, and administering career-related trainings. Her initiative, vast knowledge, and professional experiences have led to the employability of hundreds of traditionally hard-to-employ New York City residents with stigmatizing labels, mental health conditions, and criminal court barriers.

Nakita currently oversees job readiness programming for Queens Public Library, one of the largest library systems in the United States. She previously directed grant-funded young adult programs at LaGuardia Community College's Division of Adult and Continuing Education, one of the largest divisions in New York City.

Learn more at
www.linkedin.com/in/nakita-vanstory/

Nicole Washington is the founder and CEO of Fashion Counsel NYC, a style consultancy firm. She is an entrepreneur, an investor in the stock market, a certified image consultant, a fashion stylist, a freelance fashion editor, a self-professed sports junkie, and a writer. She works with ambitious, successful individuals that are ready to move up to the next level in their career and business. Nicole's youth program coaches young women on entrepreneurship, appearance, behavior, communication, and their digital imprint. She is currently working on her first book.

To connect, email her at
Nicole@fashioncounselnyc.com
or follow her on Instagram @TheBespokenMogulista

Keisha Guilford has 28 years of experience in the human services field where she specializes in structured recreation and socialization. In 2013, Keisha founded A Little Bit of Sunshine, a Brooklyn-based health and wellness company that focuses on helping people find happiness at every stage of their lives. As the CEO of ALBOS, Keisha has kept herself in positive spirits and brought together three separate business components—one-on-one counseling, workshops, and retreats.

Keisha hosts *A Little Bit of Sunshine Radio* where she discusses a variety of topics and is in the process of setting up the ALBOS store. She also offers free phone support to anyone who may need to talk. Her entrepreneurial mindset has allowed her to provide happiness to thousands of people, helping them to start living the lives they have always dreamed of.

Learn more at
www.albosnyc.com

Tamykah Anthony, born on the tiny island of Saint Vincent and the Grenadines, always had big dreams. After immigrating to America at the age of eight, Tamykah survived group homes, teenage pregnancy, and single motherhood. She graduated with honors to become an award-winning forensic toxicologist, then went on to work at Columbia University where she first became a published co-author on several scientific publications.

Tamykah appeared as a toxicologist expert on *The Dr. Oz Show* in 2019. She has since used her unique scientific background to become a tenacious entrepreneur—creating a natural product line (Xanthines All Natural Products); founding Camp Wakanda, a S.T.E.A.M. camp focused on connecting children of color to science; and her newest venture, Busy Bee Publications LLC, a full service publishing "salon" where she coupled her love of bees with her access to resources to help busy women become published authors.

Learn more at
www.busybeepublications.com

Nathan Johnson was born and raised in the county of kings—Brooklyn, New York. He served his country in the U.S. Navy and while stationed in Norfolk, Virginia, he spent four years aboard the USS Scott (DDG-995). During his tour in the Navy, he served in Operation Desert Shield. Upon his honorable discharge from the military, he relocated to Paterson, New Jersey, where he resides to this day.

Nathan worked as a receiving supervisor at Wyndham Hamilton Park Hotel and Conference Center for 12 years. As a father, grandpa, and avid Pittsburgh Steelers fan, he continues to challenge himself to be better. His desire in life is to inspire people to use adversity as fuel for growth and upward movement.

To connect, email him at
4njohnson95@gmail.com

Laura "LB" Butler is a prominent researcher within a clinical research organization specializing in infectious diseases. She has successfully blurred the lines between two incredible careers, as not only is she a top principal researcher but she is also the CEO and founder of In2itive Couture by LB Designs.

Fashionista-researcher LB is a personal stylist/shopper based in New York City who has been published in *His Favor Magazine*. LB graduated with a degree in recreation/sports medicine, but has an eye for fashion and styling her clients who range from medical professionals to journalists, musicians, clergymen, and everyone in between. From styling and personal shopping to editorial features, there isn't much that LB has yet to accomplish. She is devoted to the advancement of biomedical science, bioethics, and fashion.

To connect, email her at
in2itivecoutureLB@aol.com

Dakota Keyes has a career in education that spans 36 years with nine years within the Catholic School Diocese of Brooklyn and twenty-seven years in the New York City Department of Education. She has served as a teacher, teacher trainer, instructional specialist, assistant principal, director of early childhood education, and regional instructional specialist. Dakota has also been a principal for the past 15 years, and took PS 272 from an F to an A school.

Dakota earned a bachelor of arts in sociology with a minor in psychology from Hunter College of the City University of New York and a master of science in educational administration from Fordham University. She recently began her doctoral studies in urban education at Fordham University Lincoln Center.

She is an unapologetic Christian woman and the proud mother of three young men.

To connect, email her at
dakotakeyes1@gmail.com

Diannah "Brooklyn" Sparks is a native New Yorker and the founder of A Princess & An Heiress, a nail polish line and beauty and empowerment brand co-managed and inspired by her two daughters, Princess-Shiah and Heiress Kalani. She is also a community activist, author, educator, motivational speaker, performing artist, life coach, and a Brooklyn/New York City travel and mom blogger and influencer.

Diannah has traveled throughout the states and around the world providing humanitarian aid relief and community development in nations and cities that have been impacted by natural and man-made disasters, poverty, and other disparities.

To connect, email her at
diannahsparks@gmail.com

Tanisha Gaskin-Christie, MS, PHR is the founder of Women Who Want More, LLC, a wife, mom to three handsome boys, real estate owner, HR executive, cosmetics business owner, empowerHERcoach, and community well-being advocate. She holds a master's degree in human services administration and an undergraduate degree in human resources management/organizational development.

Tanisha's passion for helping women form clarity around getting the more that they want out of their lives is what ignited a deeper passion for her to form WWWM, LLC in July 2018. Her organization's mission is to equip women with the tools, resources, networks, trainings, outlets, wellness vehicles, and support needed in order to achieve the mental, physical, financial, and spiritual goals they have for their families and communities. The organization encourages women who want more to join the movement in creating a safe space to build and flourish by lending their unique expertise, talents, experiences, and resources.

Learn more at
www.TanishaGaskin-Christie.com

Oluwatoyin Ayanfodun holds a bachelor's degree in education from Temple University and a certification in nonprofit management from Medgar Evers College. In 2015, he was selected for the prestigious Echoing Green Fellowship Award. Born and raised in East New York, Brooklyn, Toyin is a servant leader, consultant, and nonprofit founder who has been featured on ABC 7 New York, NBC, *Forbes*, and *Huffington Post*.

In 2011, Toyin founded Tomorrow's Leaders NYC (TLNYC), the only organization in the country that provides over-age middle school students with the support services they need to develop leadership, critical thinking, and interpersonal skills. Enrolled students receive academic and family support, mentoring, and career readiness opportunities. TLNYC encourages goal setting, self-discipline, and skill development in students while tending to their social and emotional needs.

Through Ayanfodun's leadership, TLNYC has produced a variety of success stories and has seen a 95 percent grade promotion rate from enrolled middle schoolers in the program.

Learn more at
www.tlnyc.org

Tash Leath-Hamilton is a native New Yorker and celebrity intuitive life coach. Her God-given gift allows her to see a person's past, present, and potential by simply hearing their voice, reading a text, or glancing at them. Tash's mission is to inspire, empower, and positively impact people all over the globe through her intuitive ability. Her influential clients run the gamut from entertainment and sports to the business sector and includes numerous confidential A-list celebrities, international luminaries, and Fortune 500 executives.

Tash is a recurring guest on *The Quicksilva Show with Dominique Da Diva*, a syndicated show on Radio One. She has also been featured on Sirius XM's *The Clay Cane Show*, *The Jenny McCarthy Show*, *Angela Yee's Lip Service*, the TV One show *For My Man*, and *The Quiet Storm with Lenny Green* on 107.5 WBLS and Condé Nast. She resides in the tri-state area with her husband.

Learn more at
www.TalkToTash.com

Sue Fearless was born and raised in Washington Heights in the heart of New York City. Sue has been able to embody the soul, culture, and diversity of New York City as a child of Latino parents (her father was from the Dominican Republic and her single mother is of Puerto Rican descent). Sue is a master of finance graduate and has two children who motivate and empower her daily. She has grown successfully in her career in finance, management, and consulting. Sue also has a career in promoting and event planning.

Sue is passionate about empowering and mentoring young ladies and women through her organization, FEARLESS WOMEN, LLC. She is creating a women's conference and movement that uplifts and empowers women in the tri-state area and around the country. Through her podcast, *The Fearless Show*, Sue provides a platform for others to use their voices to inspire.

Learn more at
www.Fearless-Women.com

Melissa Cisco has practiced law for over twenty years. She earned a bachelor of arts in criminal justice from the University at Albany in 1991 and a law degree with honors from the District of Columbia School in 1996. In 2008, Melissa joined the New York City Department of Education (DOE) as a special education teacher and earned two masters in education. As the college and career advisor and international studies coordinator, she organized trips for inner-city youth and traveled with students to Africa, Europe, and South America.

Melissa recently transitioned into a new role within the DOE as the director of communications for the Division of School Climate and Wellness. She enjoys traveling, reading, cooking, decorating, house hunting, and mentoring youth.

To connect, email her at
melissagcisco@gmail.com

Michelle Jenkins is an education change agent whose goals are to create change by mastering teaching in higher education, educating prospective early childhood educators, and building a bridge between society's rapid changes and the miseducation of students. She is employed as an early childhood teacher and program site coordinator for the Boys & Girls Clubs of the Capital Area in partnership with the Albany City School District. Michelle is a co-founder of East New York Kids, Inc., a nonprofit organization that provides resources and annual activities throughout communities.

Michelle's passion for learning and teaching has earned her an associates of arts in teacher education, a bachelor of arts in early childhood special education, a master of science in sociology with an emphasis in education, and she is finalizing her studies toward a master of science in special education and literacy. Michelle has received multiple awards and honors from Medgar Evers College for her academic excellence.

To connect, email her at
michellejenkins92@gmail.com

Lakeasha Williams is a Brooklyn native who is enthusiastic about working in a community that she loves. She is a social justice educational leader with over twenty years of experience as a paraprofessional, classroom teacher, staff developer, assistant principal, special education administrator (Districts 17, 18, 22), and TDEC (principal coach) for District 17. Her greatest strengths include instructional leadership, school improvement action plans, data driven culture, differentiated professional development, community engagement, family empowerment initiatives, and meeting all school-wide compliance mandates. Lakeasha is dedicated to working collaboratively with her school community, engaging all key stakeholders to meet and exceed the school goals.

Lakeasha was recently featured on ABC 7, WPIX 11, NowThis Politics, and RAI (the Italian broadcasting corporation) for her brown girls empowerment activity with her fifth grade girls. Lakeasha continues to further develop her professional acumen. She looks forward to completing her PhD program in educational leadership.

Learn more at
www.brickhouseunlimited.com

Shatema Reedy is a newly developed entrepreneur whose business, HYSC (Here's Your Second Chance), is geared toward career development through seminars, job fair events, and resume writing. Born and raised in Brooklyn, New York, Ms. Reedy has worked in career development and recruitment for nonprofit organizations such as Goodwill Industries of Greater NY & Northern NJ for ten years. She currently co-teaches the clerk academy as a sales and services associate instructor for the United States Postal Service. Shatema recently received a professional training webinar certification through Life Path and Coaching Solutions.

Above all, Shatema serves as a cleric in her local ministry in Brooklyn, New York, and continues to raise her vibrant and energetic six-year-old daughter, Shayla.

Learn more at
www.facebook.com/hyscinfo

Deidra Towns is a trauma-informed thought leader who speaks, writes, and facilitates transformative leadership development, mindset mastery, and joyful well-being. She coaches emerging leaders whose work is creating a new paradigm based on love, justice, and freedom. Deidra is also a master teacher of the Stress Reset Methodology.

At the intersection of her passion for social justice and her lifelong inclination to curate sacred wisdom is the substance of her mission to be a catalyst for folks to heal their trauma, harmonize their shadows, and amplify love in the world.

Deidra is a recovered "good girl" who mothered three children into adulthood. When she's not working, you'll find her nerding out on movies, music, and pleasure principles.

Learn more at
www.DeidraTowns.com

Mecca Nelson is the CEO of Mecca's City of Wholeness and founder of The YOMA Method (a revolutionary practice of Vinyasa yoga, mixed martial arts, and meditation). A number one bestselling author, Mecca is also a mother, motivational speaker, contract vendor with the Department of Education, an advocate, and the chairperson of Humble Haitian Warrior Inc., a nonprofit 501(c)(3).

As a Gold Star spouse, Mecca began to train in martial arts to deal with the death of her husband. She combined yoga, martial arts, and meditation to offer a comprehensive model of wellness, creating a balanced, empowering, and healing practice for all ages. She also facilitates workshops on cultivating healthy relationships between parents and children, self-care, massage techniques, professional development, and consultant work.

YOMA has been mentioned in *The Daily Beast* and featured as the top story in *The Haitian Times*, NYC Veterans Source, and more.

Learn more at
www.yomamethod.com

Cindy Brown was born and raised in Trinidad and Tobago. She migrated to the United Stated in 1998 to acquire her bachelor of arts at Medgar Evers College. In 2001, she was crowned Miss Medgar Evers College for her famous monologue performance of Sojourner Truth's Ain't I a Woman? One of Ms. Brown's many accolades at Medgar Evers College was a feature in *Ebony* magazine entitled "The College Queen." Ms. Brown has performed at venues such as the Jamaica Chamber of Commerce, Concord Baptist Church, and her alma mater, Medgar Evers College. Ms. Brown acquired her master of business from Monroe College in 2009 and is the founder of Sisters of Excellence.

Ms. Brown is currently a small business banker who covers the Long Island Market with Bank of America. She is the proud mother of a fifteen-year-old son who enjoys basketball and playing the piano.

Learn more at
www.sistersofexcellence.com

Denise Kennedy is an entrepreneur who believes that her brain functions more efficiently on the creative side of the entrepreneur sphere. She is the CEO and owner of Pocket of Hope (which means hope for love, peace, salvation, and healing), a Christian towel and clothing company. Pocket of Hope was born out of Denise's desire to help people who have life-threatening illnesses.

Denise is a novice poet who started writing poetry in 2018 to relate to others who were also on a journey of healing. She believes that poetry comes from the soul. She will publish her book of poetry in the near future.

Denise's favorite Scripture is Jeremiah 29:11 NKJV: "For I know the thoughts that I think toward you, says the Lord, thoughts of peace and not of evil, to give you a future and a hope."

Learn more at
www.pocketofhope.org

Kelvin Weathers is a gifted, devoted, empowering, and inspiring transformational speaker, minister, educational consultant, and mentor. He has spoken to youth, adults, and other diverse audiences for the past 17 years.

Kelvin acquired his associate of arts from Houston Community College and his bachelor of arts from Texas Southern University. He is the oldest of five children and resides in Houston, Texas, with his wife, Allyson.

To connect, email him at
kelvinlw@hotmail.com

Nkechi Ogbodo was born in Nigeria. She earned a bachelor of arts in political science from Lehman College in Bronx, New York, and a master of arts in international relations from The City College of the City University of New York. She is president and founder of Kechie's Project Inc., a 501(c)(3) nonprofit organization that empowers girls and boys of color through education and mentoring. In addition to Kechie's Project, Nkechi has vast experience in the fashion industry and has worked for renowned luxury retailers and brands.

Nkechi is currently a style advisor at Saks Fifth Avenue where she is one of the top producing style advisors, generating over one million dollars in yearly sales.

To connect, email her at
kechie11@gmail.com

Michelle Richburg has developed a specialized niche in the financial services industry as a "Banker for the Stars" with a strong reputation for competence, efficiency, and creativity. Over the span of nearly 30 years, her client list has included high-profile professional athletes, entertainers, and business leaders.

As owner, president, and CEO of Richburg Enterprises, Ms. Richburg shares her special skills with the world and provides services that did not exist in the market. Her brand of hands-on, client-centered work put an innovative and unique spin on every aspect of business administration, including insurance coverage, wealth management, accounting, and other specialty areas.

Michelle graduated from Mercy College with a BS in business administration and has completed training programs in wealth management, marketing management, total quality management, and banking. She is a native of White Plains, New York, and a lifelong member of Saint Frances AME Zion Church in Port Chester, New York.

Learn more at LinkedIn
@michellerichburg

CPSIA information can be obtained
at www.ICGtesting.com
Printed in the USA
BVHW041442260821
615328BV00014B/558